The Chelsea Football Book No. 4

THE CHELSEA FOOTBALL BOOK

No. 4

Edited by Albert Sewell

STANLEY PAUL, LONDON

STANLEY PAUL & CO LTD
3 Fitzroy Square, London W1

AN IMPRINT OF THE HUTCHINSON GROUP

London Melbourne Sydney Auckland
Wellington Johannesburg Cape Town
and agencies throughout the world

First Published 1973

This book has been set in Baskerville, printed in Great Britain by offset litho by Flarepath Printers Ltd., St. Albans, Herts. and bound by William Brendon of Tiptree, Essex

ISBN 0 09 117190 3

Contents

These Changing Times

By BRIAN MEARS
(Chairman of Chelsea)

THE face of Football is changing rapidly. Last season brought a new disciplinary procedure to the game; another experiment, one that could have far-reaching effects, was with closed-circuit television; and the August 25 start is a pointer to future seasons running from the beginning of September to the end of May.

Nowhere am I more aware of change than at Stamford Bridge, where we embarked last year on a £5½ million redevelopment programme to be completed during the seventies. Unfortunately, a lot of inconvenience, to Club, Players and Supporters, particularly last season, has also had to be written into the cost of progress.

We all know that lack of atmosphere at Stamford Bridge is something Chelsea players have needed to live with down the years. The fact that we are taking spectacular steps to remedy this meant that, temporarily, still less atmosphere could be generated last winter in a three-sided stadium, and one result was that we had one of our most disappointing seasons since the war. It hit all the harder, coming after two Cup successes and a Final appearance in the three previous years.

Dave Sexton, who struggled all season with vast injury problems, summed up the additional handicap caused by rebuilding when he said: 'There is no point in denying that it has been a strain on us. We've had to shuffle around all the time, with the injured treated in one place and the main squad at Mitcham. The construction has been like having the builders in your own home for a year. You can tolerate it when things are going well, but it adds to the irritation when things go wrong.'

Let's hope the 'depression' of last season is far, far behind us as we begin 1973–74. Soon the new, two-tier East Stand, which

Stamford Bridge as it was East side before Chelsea's mammoth rebuilding programme began in 1972.

Stamford Bridge as it will be—the 'Concorde of the Fulham Road'—when redevelopment is completed.

will seat 12,000 compared with the 6,000 capacity of its predecessor, will come into use, and a first-phase milestone will have been reached.

By the time the whole exciting redevelopment project is completed, Stamford Bridge will be covered on all sides and we shall have a stadium capable of seating 60,000. There will be restaurants, a banqueting room, 156 private viewing boxes, electric information scoreboard, a new floodlighting system, vice-presidents' club, increased bar and toilet accommodation.

All that is for our spectators. On the playing side we shall have, for the first time in our history, a real football stadium for a home, with the surrounding greyhound track removed, with the elliptical ends behind both goals squared up to bring the fans nearer to the action, and with covered stands all round to provide the sort of crowd atmosphere we have always longed for and which our players previously experienced only when they went to grounds like Anfield, Old Trafford, Highbury and White Hart Lane. They will also have the best of modern dressing-room and medical-room facilities and a large indoor practice area. For our administrative staff magnificent accommodation, providing the best possible working conditions, will be located in the new main stand. In one respect most Football League clubs have made no progress over the past ten, twenty, fifty years—or, indeed, since the game began. We are still using our stadia in an earning capacity for only 25–30 days in the year. Today's economics demand that they are put to far greater use. How we harness our earning power to maximum advantage is something to which we are giving the greatest thought at Chelsea. Most certainly ways and means of doing so need to be found. Naturally, we hope our potentially all-seater arena will be considered for European Finals and F.A. Cup semi-finals. Stamford Bridge could, perhaps, be a future venue for major boxing events, but these are all 'occasional possibilities' rather than something to be regarded as a source of *regular* revenue, which is what we must look for. I would like to think the 'new' Stamford Bridge will have big earning potential in its off-the-field activities, with a restaurant open to the public for lunch and dinner every day of the week and a banqueting hall that should appeal to industry as a conference centre so near to London's West End.

At a totally different tangent, one change I would like to see within the present framework of the game concerns the eligibility of transferred players for Cup-ties. Two seasons ago, you will recall, Chelsea paid their record fee for Steve Kember from

Brian Mears at his Richmond home, twenty minutes' drive from his football home, Stamford Bridge.

Crystal Palace. We signed him in the September, but it was a whole year before he could play for us in the League Cup. The reason: when he came to us, he was already Cup-tied for the rest of that season with Palace. At about the same time we signed Chris Garland from Bristol City, but whereas Kember had to sit and watch us go all the way to the 1972 League Cup Final at Wembley, Garland was able to play for us because, by chance, injury had prevented his appearing for his previous club in their opening League Cup-tie that season.

We were in a similar position last season when we signed Bill Garner from Southend the day after he had played against us in the second round of the League Cup. It becomes increasingly important for Football to realise its part in the business of public entertainment. We must keep pace with the times and, as I see it, clubs do not pay six-figure transfer fees to have players ruled out of big matches by possibly outdated regulations.

I believe the time has come to revise the rule which Cup-ties a player to one club for a whole season. Certainly, there remains the need for safeguard against clubs buying themselves greater strength for semi-finals and Finals, so I suggest that a transferred player, if Cup-tied with his previous team, should remain so for two further rounds. Then let him become eligible for his new club.

There was a precedent in season 1957–58. Manchester United, decimated by the Munich air crash and desperately rebuilding a team to complete the season, were given special dispensation to field an already Cup-tied player (Stan Crowther from Aston Villa) in their F.A. Cup side which reached Wembley. Let us hope Football will never again suffer a tragedy producing such circumstances. Equally, I would like to think that before very much longer players are allowed to appear for more than one club in Cup football in the same season. Will it be the Football League Cup or the FA Cup, I wonder, that gives the lead?

Twelve of the Best

By JOHN HOLLINS

I CAN still remember the first day I arrived at Chelsea—and that's not bad considering it was twelve years ago! It was the day the first team reported back for pre-season training. They were all sun-tanned and there I was, a small 15-year-old, as white as a sheet.

That morning I found myself training with Peter Bonetti and Ron Tindall. I had to cross the ball for Ron to try and head it in. At that time he was the club's best header and Peter, of course, was already one of the game's top goalkeepers. In such company I couldn't have had a better start. But then, all the experienced players at the club were very helpful, offering good advice and no one trying to knock the new boy down. For me, it was like a dream come true.

Chelsea's professionals trained at Ewell in those days and the juniors at Hendon. But I didn't stay at Hendon long. An office-boy was needed at Stamford Bridge and, without volunteering, I got the job.

I was upset at the time because I didn't want to leave the other lads at Hendon, but that move was a blessing in disguise. I trained with the first team and reserves and began to get a close insight into what went on at the club.

It wasn't all roses, though. I still had to carry out the office-boy duties. I didn't arrive home at Guildford most evenings until gone 6.30 p.m. And I wasn't paid any more than the other apprentices.

I was a winger when I came here and people used to say: 'Oh, he'll never make it.' But Dick Foss, manager of the Youth scheme in those days, switched me to half-back—and I never looked back. In the new role I captained Chelsea's juniors before getting a break in the reserves.

I had been a full professional only two months when Tommy Docherty decided to blood me in a League Cup-tie away to

Above: Skipper John leads Chelsea into action at Southampton last year.

Below: Up and at 'em—Hollins beats the tackle to get in his shot against Orient.

Up above 'em—John takes on Arsenal hard men Peter Storey and Alan Ball in last season's sixth round FA Cup-tie.

Swindon Town. That was in September 1963. It wasn't a very happy beginning because Swindon won 3–0. But the following March I found myself making my First Division début at Stoke against the great Jimmy McIlroy. We lost 2–0, but my name was on the next team-sheet at home to Fulham . . . facing Johnny Haynes. Again Chelsea went down, and although I went back

Opposite: Away from the action, John gets down to some football homework, signing magazines, photographs and autograph books.

into the reserves, the experience of playing at seventeen on the same field as McIlroy and Haynes was invaluable.

It certainly came in handy when I was a last-minute selection for Chelsea's summer tour of the West Indies. Frank Upton had been injured towards the end of the season and I was called up as his replacement.

That was the turning point of my career. We played Wolves five times during that 1964 trip and the experience set me up just right. By sheer coincidence Chelsea's first match of the new season was away to Wolves. We won 3–0.

Of that line-up Peter Bonetti, Eddie McCreadie, Marvin Hinton and Ron Harris are still playing colleagues of mine at The Bridge. Ken Shellito, who was right-back behind me that day, is still here as well, of course as Youth team manager.

Blonde Australian Sally Burnham, 16-year-old farmer's daughter from Moss Vale, New South Wales, saw Chelsea on TV 'down under' and became an instant fan. She saved £350 to make the 12,000 mile trip to come and see them play—and looked in at the training ground with her London pen-friend Paula Bright to meet the players. John Hollins provided a 'tartan-tammied hello' and this happy picture for Sally to take home. She said: 'To speak to the Chelsea team was a terrific thrill. I never believed it would happen to me. My knees were knocking'.

For some reason or other, which no one at the club can explain, Chelsea have usually been slow starters in the League. But not in 1964.

We went the first ten games without defeat (seven wins, three draws) but the end of the run came at Stamford Bridge in front of a full-house 60,000. The opposition? Manchester United, complete with Bobby Charlton, Denis Law and a young George Best. We went down 2–0 and Best scored the first goal. It took us half the first half to realise that we were playing that day. But we were a young side, learning from every game.

For the first time in 13 years, Chelsea fought their way through to the FA Cup semi-finals that season. We met Liverpool at

Opposite: Footballer of the Month! Hollins won the *Evening Standard* award for October 1972, and the prize, presented by Dave Sexton is an inscribed silver salver and two magnums of champagne.

Villa Park, where what we all thought was a good goal by John Mortimore from a corner was disallowed. Liverpool beat us 2–0, but nine days later we picked up the League Cup—a comparatively minor competition in those days—as a consolation.

We were cup-fighting in a big way again the following season. Once more we reached the semi-finals, but again we went no further. Sheffield Wednesday was the club to send us spinning from the competition this time. But, of course, the Villa Park semi-final bogey was laid the next year, 1967, although it wasn't until 1970 that the Blues at last lifted the FA Cup.

There was a remarkable similarity between the beaten Chelsea side of 1965 and the triumphant one of five years later. Both had strength at the back and the ability to score goals out of nowhere. The 1970 side accomplished what was nearly achieved in 1965. The difference was that we had experience as an ally in the final with Leeds. Had the earlier team achieved a big success, most of us might still have been together now. But it wasn't to be.

Why have Chelsea produced that little bit extra in cup-ties, while lacking consistency in the League? I think the injury problems we had killed off our championship chances over the past two or three seasons.

Tackling the top shot. Hollins challenges West Ham's 'Pop' Robson, leading First Division goalscorer last season.

My great ambition is to play in a Chelsea championship side. I thought we would be in with a big chance last time, but again it was only in cup competitions that we struck anything like our real form. The only excuse I can offer is the fact that we were heavily hit by injuries.

We had a terrific boost in December when Ian Hutchinson returned after a long absence. His presence brought a new surge of enthusiasm to the side—but suddenly he was out again. At various times Peter Bonetti, Eddie McCreadie, Chris Garland, John Dempsey, Micky Droy, Dave Webb, Bill Garner and Peter Houseman all joined Hutch on the injured list. It was only our tremendous strength in depth that enabled us to keep going as well as we did.

Another reason put forward for Chelsea's indifferent League performances was that with the rebuilding of Stamford Bridge we'd lost the advantage of playing at home. I don't agree entirely. You can always hear the Shed and their encouragement is

Who's that unlikely goalkeeper throwing the ball over John Hollins? The clue is in the No. 7 stocking tab . . . and the answer is Peter Lorimer, who became emergency 'keeper for Leeds in last season's opening game after David Harvey was carried off with concussion.

tremendous. But with one side of the ground closed we did lose some atmosphere . . . and concentration. At times it was like playing on a park on a Sunday morning. But thinking long-term, I'd say it's a small price to pay while Stamford Bridge is being turned into a marvellous stadium of the future.

At grounds like Highbury, Anfield and White Hart Lane, where the play is close to the terraces, no player wants to make a mistake. And I think this definitely makes us play better, and is one reason why Chelsea are a hard side to beat away from home. What's more, we like people to come at us. We can soak up the pressure, break suddenly and score.

Two matches that stand out in my memory for the part played by the Stamford Bridge crowd are the Fairs Cup-tie against

AC Milan in the 1965–66 season and the European Cup-Winners' Cup match with Belgian club, Bruges, in the 1970–71 quarter-final.

The night we played Milan here was electric—60,000 inside, thousands locked out and fans sitting all round the greyhound track. The support was fantastic. I'm sure it was worth a goal start. We had lost the first leg 2–1 in Italy, won the second here by the same score, then drew the play-off 1–1 back in Milan and went through to the next round by the spin of a coin.

The Bruges battle was just as dramatic. We'd lost 2–0 in Belgium and were up against it in the second leg. But again the Chelsea crowd lifted us. When the chants are echoing from all corners of the ground, you chase balls you've little hope of

getting; because you are being urged on, your legs just keep running.

With support like that, it was no surprise that we drew level with Bruges and then won the tie in extra time. I've tasted success in three Chelsea Cup-winning teams, with England Youth and Under-23 caps and in one full international against Spain at Wembley six years ago.

I've set my sights on Munich next year. It's got to be that World Cup or bust for me. Last time I was in the original 40 for Mexico, but I didn't make the final party, so I must try to play my best football this season. Consistency is the thing; with Sir Alf it's no good being a five-minute wonder. He has got to consider you dependable.

I am often asked about our training schedule at Chelsea and just what we do between one Saturday and the next. Perhaps this will give you some idea.

If everything has gone all right on Saturday we usually have Monday off. On Tuesday we report to the training ground at Mitcham, where we start the morning with some exercises and sprint routines to limber up.

Then Dave Sexton settles down to analysing the tactical things that went right—or wrong—in the previous game.

Once we have established what we need to polish up—perhaps throw-in moves, corner-kicks or similar deadball situations—we hammer away at them until we are satisfied.

Passing practice is next, and then we all pile into a van to Epsom Downs for a four-mile cross country run. Peter Bonetti, John Boyle and Peter Houseman usually set the pace. Me? I'm a fair bet to finish fourth or fifth. And, thankfully, that's it for the day.

Wednesday is 'fun morning'. It's indoor work at Roehampton with gym games followed by five-a-side matches. The hardest work of the week is 'doggies'. That involves timed-sprints up and down the gym—and believe me when that's over we're all dog-tired! We finish the session with some squash, swimming or a sauna bath.

On Thursday it's back to Mitcham for more sprinting and tactical talk-ins. Dave Sexton discusses our opponents and gives us our instructions and duties for the coming game.

Friday we report to The Bridge for a few last sprints and exercises, but as it's so near the match this is only a light session. We play a short five-a-side and finally Dave Sexton brushes us up on the individual tasks ahead of us next day.

We all have different habits on Saturdays. If we are playing

What's the joke, chaps? John and Bobby Charlton prove there's still time for a smile in the serious business of modern football at top level.

at home I usually rise at about 9 a.m. and have a light breakfast of cereal, toast and tea. I leave home two hours later to arrive at our Gloucester Road hotel meeting place by noon.

I'm not a great eater on match-days. Lunch for me is some more toast. But most of the others have a steak, while Ossie and Huddie can sometimes even manage two! After the meal we watch the lunch-time football programmes on TV.

Then it's off to the ground. We arrive at about 1.30 p.m. and by two o'clock we are shutting ourselves away in the dressing-room. We change and then go into the gym (opposite the present make-shift dressing-room) where Dave gives his final talk-in. Sometimes he says he hasn't slept all night but instead has dreamed up new tactical plans for us to run through.

Usually we just practise one or two things again to make sure we have got them off pat. Back in the dressing-room the tension builds up. Webbie's always the last to get ready. Before the lunch-time meeting routine was introduced you could always rely on him turning up late. He used to stroll in, about twenty minutes before the kick-off, change and trot out.

I couldn't do that. I've got to be there early to check whether my boots are right and to give myself plenty of time to get changed. John Dempsey is a bit of a joker by nature, but even he is quiet as the kick-off gets nearer. Meanwhile, Dave Sexton is moving among us, quietly boosting confidence all round.

We've practically reached the half-way line by the time Webbie gets out. Last again! Ossie won't walk directly behind Peter Bonetti but otherwise there are no longer any real superstitions in the team.

I enjoyed my spell as Chelsea captain last season. Shouting has long been part of my game, so offering encouragement comes easily. But a good captain, in my opinion, must be able to chastise as well—to have a quiet word or gesture to a colleague when necessary. It doesn't take much, because professional players know only too well when they've made a mess of something.

At half time we have a quick discussion on the first 45 minutes. If things are going smoothly we aim to continue along the same lines, but if we are in trouble we may revise our plans. About ten minutes into the second half the captain looks across to the bench to see if any changes are wanted.

But it isn't often that Dave Sexton makes a substitution, unless it's forced by injury. He likes to stick with the team he has selected. After all last season's injuries I just hope he's able to do that a lot more often in 1973–74.

Magical Moments in the FA Cup

Editor Albert Sewell completes a 25-season association with Chelsea in 1973-74. Here he delves back through those years and recaptures some of the Club's MAGICAL MOMENTS IN THE FA CUP.

We all have different memories of our 'first Chelsea goal', the one that stands out as the real starting point in our affection for the Blues. Mine was on a bitterly cold day in January 1950 . . . Chelsea at home to Newcastle United in the fourth round of the F.A. Cup. Today the match would never have been played, because the pitch was frozen solid, but in those days the show went on, and what a show it was by Chelsea.

That was long before the coaches inflicted the modern midfield mania on the game. Attack meant five forwards up, plus a wing-half or two in close support, with wingers on both flanks to make sure that the full width of the pitch was used. The fans couldn't resist that sort of football; never mind the deep-freeze temperature, 64,644 packed Stamford Bridge that day, and with Newcastle fielding an attack of Tommy Walker, George Robledo, Jackie Milburn, George Hannah and Bobby Mitchell, they knew that nothing less than the best would do from Chelsea's defence.

On the morning of the tie Chelsea were hit by a blow as cruel as the conditions. John Harris, captain, centre-half and cornerstone of the defence, failed a test on the right ankle he had twisted the previous week at Fulham, and his understudy was Jack Saunders, a craggy North-easterner from Middlesbrough, making only his second senior appearance. Against a marksman of Milburn's reputation, the test could not have been greater. Neither could Chelsea's start as, before Newcastle goalkeeper Jack Fairbrother could get a proper feel of the ball, Hugh Billington hammered home a 20-yarder. A lovely move across the field from left to right ended with Billington scoring a second, but for individual brilliance the third, seven minutes from time, belonged in the Chelsea gallery of truly great solo goals.

I see it now almost as clearly as I did then, scored by Bobby Campbell, a dark-haired winger who had been signed by Billy Birrell from Falkirk in May 1947—one of the many Scottish players Birrell brought to Stamford Bridge. Speed and tenacity were just two of Campbell's many qualities. In scoring that day, he showed an abundance of both, as well as an ice-skater's sense of balance in the light rubber boots to which he had changed at half-time to increase manoeuvrability on the hard, slippery pitch.

Seldom has a ball left one goalmouth and reached the net at the other end in so few seconds. Now trainer-coach of Bristol Rovers, Campbell remembers it well: 'With 15 minutes left Hughie Billington, who had scored those two first-half goals,

What a shot! This was the spectacular FA Cup goal by Roy Bentley (extreme right) against Manchester United in the sixth round in 1950.

Harry Medhurst, then Chelsea's goalkeeper and now the club's trainer, is down and Chelsea are out. Freddie Cox has shot the only goal of the 1950 semi-final replay at Tottenham . . . and more than 20 years later Chelsea are still seeking FA Cup revenge against Arsenal.

A goal fit to win any cup-tie—but it didn't work out like that. Peter Osgood opens the scoring in the sixth round at home to Arsenal last March. It was voted 'Goal of the Season' in the BBC Match of the Day competition for which there was 215,000 entries.

Chelsea's last FA Cup goal . . . until the start of another Wembley bid in January 1974. Peter Houseman (No. 11) has headed the ball past Arsenal 'keeper Bob Wilson to open the scoring in last season's sixth round replay at Highbury.

was injured. No substitutes then, of course; we were down to ten men and Newcastle, sensing that if they got one back they might get two, hit us with everything.

'They charged Harry Medhurst over the line for a corner and sent everyone bar their 'keeper into our box. I was all alone near the half-way line. Over came the corner. Roy Bentley cleared the ball out to me. I turned and kicked it over the centre line, then ran like hell with everyone in pursuit about 50 yards behind. Fairbrother came at me, but I toe-ended the ball past him. That made the result three–nil, and the stadium absolutely rocked. I'll never forget it. As the ball hit the net there were still only three players in the Newcastle half, Fairbrother, the big centre-half Frank Brennan and myself.'

That was the first of my 'most memorable Chelsea goals'. The same season, two rounds later, came another. Between times, in Round 5, Chesterfield had been beaten 3–0 in a replay at The Bridge, putting Chelsea in the quarter-final against Championship leaders Manchester United, again at home, with 70,362 paying record receipts of £10,032. There was stature all over the field as the teams lined up: Chelsea—Harry Medhurst, Danny Winter, Bill Hughes; Ken Armstrong, John Harris, Frank Mitchell; Billy Gray, Reg Williams, Roy Bentley, Hugh Billington, Bobby Campbell. Manchester United—Jack Crompton; Johnny Carey, John Aston, Jack Warner, Allenby Chilton, Henry Cockburn; Jimmy Delaney, Johnny Downie, Jack Rowley, Stan Pearson and Charlie Mitten.

Again, as against Newcastle, Chelsea had the tonic of a snap goal, scored in the sixth minute when Campbell hit Billington's return pass sweetly past Crompton. The real clincher came twenty minutes from time—one of Roy Bentley's most spectacular shots for the club. The build-up was five-star, too, with Winter pushing a top-spinner along the right touchline to Bentley, who immediately moved the ball on to Gray. His cute back-heel threw United's defence off balance and Bentley, advancing unchallenged for several paces, sent a left-footer high into the net for the goal of the round.

Matches against Leeds United have been conspicuous on Chelsea's menu of post-war Cup-ties, and the fifth round of season 1951–52 provided a tie that went through two gruelling encounters to a third meeting. Leeds were then sixth from the top of the Second Division, Chelsea fifth from bottom of the First, and two minutes after Jimmy Milburn had opened the scoring at Elland Road, 18-year-old Bobby Smith scored a welcome equaliser . . . in borrowed boots. Travelling overnight

AUSTIN

from his Army unit in Hampshire, he mislaid his own, so a pair size $8\frac{1}{2}$ belonging to Jack Saunders, were rushed North from Stamford Bridge.

The replay four days later also ended one-all, Irish International Jimmy D'Arcy saving Chelsea with a goal two minutes from the end of normal time. Villa Park the following Monday afternoon was the venue of the play-off and, as often happens in marathon Cup-ties, it ended with one side winning so convincingly as to leave one bewildered by all the earlier equality. Roy Bentley got Chelsea sharply off the mark with a header, and after Leeds replied Bobby Smith, still wearing the 'wrong' boots, scored three goals in 17 minutes—his first Chelsea hat-trick—in a 5–1 victory.

In the summer of 1953 Ted Drake succeeded Billy Birrell at Stamford Bridge, and Chelsea's first FA Cup-tie under the new manager produced one of the greatest rallies in the competition's history. In the third round at the Baseball Ground, Chelsea were losing 1–4 to Derby County with twenty minutes left. Then, in an incredible eight minutes (71–79 mins), Eric Parsons, Ken Armstrong and Johnny McNichol all scored, and that 4–4 result remains the highest-scoring FA Cup draw Chelsea have ever played.

Parsons won the replay with the only goal in extra time, which set up Chelsea for a fourth round tie against West Bromwich Albion that exceeded the previous year's marathon with Leeds. It stretched to four matches over twelve days, and a League fixture against Sunderland was sandwiched in the middle. Red-shirted Chelsea (yes, those were the second colours then, as they became again last season) drew the first game against Albion 1–1 at The Bridge, Roy Bentley shooting the equaliser before half-time. Next came two gruelling, goalless hours at The Hawthorns. The third meeting, at Villa Park, looked like going West Bromwich's way when they scored fifteen minutes from time, but almost at once Bentley lobbed the match-saver, and in extra time Miles Spector, an 18-year-old Hendon Grammar School boy newly promoted from Chelsea's 'A' side, twice went close to winning the tie.

Again a landslide ended the argument, for in the third replay at Highbury Chelsea triumphed 4–0. Such a margin never looked likely when Ken Armstrong had a 30th-minute penalty saved—John Harris, the regular spot-kicker, was in bed with flu—but Bentley broke the deadlock nine minutes after half time, Parsons shot the second, Bentley headed No. 3 and Campbell's fourth completed the rout in a tie that, over the

The greatest picture of all in nearly 70 years of FA Cup action by Chelsea, as David Webb heads the goal that beat Leeds in the 1970 Final replay at Old Trafford.

four episodes, was watched by 158,417 spectators. Too bad, though, that Birmingham were waiting to pick off the exhausted winners by another four–nil at Stamford Bridge only three days later.

In season 1955–56 which opened with Chelsea as League Champions, they added the longest tie in their history to the ever-enriching fabric of the FA Cup. It was against Burnley in the fourth round and began with a 1–1 draw in the dour setting of Turf Moor. Eric Parsons' equaliser did not come until the last six minutes, setting Chelsea on the way to their 'marathon of marathons'. The Stamford Bridge replay also resulted 1–1 after Frank Blunstone gave Chelsea the lead. Next stop was Birmingham's ground at St. Andrew's, where Chelsea twice recovered—through Peter Sillett (penalty) and Roy Bentley—to draw 2–2, again after extra time. Back to London for the fourth stage, resulting 0–0 after two hours at Arsenal Stadium, and finally, two days later at Tottenham, Burnley were cracked 2–0, scorers Ron Tindall and Jim Lewis. In the moment of victory, Ted Drake had some strong words to say about a club being required to pack five hard Cup matches—as they had all been against Burnley—into 19 days, with two other League games thrown in during the same hectic spell. So by the time Chelsea visited Everton in the fifth round only three days after nailing Burnley, they were playing their eighth testing match in 22 mid-winter days from 28 January–18 February. Not surprisingly, Bentley and his weary warriors were not up to the task at Goodison Park, where Chelsea went out by the only goal.

From the middle fifties we switch to the middle sixties and, under Tommy Docherty's boisterous command, the most exciting period yet in Chelsea's pursuit of the FA Cup, with a hat-trick of semi-final appearances in 1965–66–67, all at Villa Park. With Chelsea leading the Championship and 3–2 ahead after the first leg of the League Cup Final, they were candidates for possible triple triumph when they met Liverpool in the FA Cup semi-final. The whole destiny of the club under Docherty might have been different if centre-half John Mortimore's header from a corner had been allowed, but the referee decided that he had impeded goalkeeper Tommy Lawrence, and Liverpool took the Wembley place with second half goals by Thompson and Stevenson (penalty). Winning the League Cup (still then in its pre-Wembley days) was minimum compensation for the season's mammoth all-round effort.

By way of revenge, Chelsea started the 1965–66 FA Cup with a third round win 2–1 away to Liverpool and followed by beating

Not long, let's hope, before Chairman Brian Mears is once again placing the FA Cup in Chelsea's trophy cabinet, as he was doing here in 1970.

Leeds in Round 4 at The Bridge. They did it with Bobby Tambling's eighth-minute goal and 82 minutes of unyielding defence and, having eliminated teams of that calibre, Chelsea were confident, when they got to the semi-final, that the last barrier to Wembley—Sheffield Wednesday, fourth from bottom of the First Division table—would fall. But the Villa Park jinx was at work again. Chelsea never came to terms with the mud-heap conditions, Wednesday did . . . and for the second successive year we trailed home with tails down, beaten two–nil at the last stop before Wembley. It was the first and last time Chelsea wore blue-and-black striped Inter-Milan type shirts, black shorts and socks.

It just had to be third time lucky, didn't it, when Tommy Docherty took Chelsea back to Villa's ground for the 1967 semi-final against Leeds? The previous October Docherty had paid Chelsea's first £100,000 transfer fee to buy Tony Hateley from

Aston Villa. By the following June the big fellow had left Stamford Bridge for Liverpool and Chelsea got back all but £5,000 of their outlay. Hateley's supreme moment in his eight months with Chelsea came in the semi-final on his old ground, when he rose to Charlie Cooke's centre from the left and headed past Sprake. With a minute to go and Chelsea hanging on by their finger-nails, Leeds were awarded a free-kick just outside the box. Giles played it short to Lorimer who lashed a 20-yarder unstoppably past Peter Bonetti, and Chelsea hearts sank. The Villa Park hoodoo had struck again . . . but no, referee Ken Burns disallowed the goal, ruling that Leeds had taken the free-kick before he was ready. On that hairline decision Chelsea conquered a semi-final jinx that had hung over them since 1920; they were at Wembley for the FA Cup Final for the first time; but getting there and winning there were vastly different things and, come the big day, Tottenham won 2–1 against opponents well below their best.

The Blues took three more years to reach the Final again. Then at last in 1970, in the third season of Dave Sexton's managership, came the magic finish. For the only time, Wembley failed to produce a winner, with first Peter Houseman and, in the closing minutes of normal time, Ian Hutchinson answering Leeds goals to make the result 2–2 after extra time. In the replay at Old Trafford, 18 days later, Leeds once more went ahead, but Peter Bonetti, superb at Wembley, became a hero again as he battled on, virtually on one leg, after injuring his left knee. Twelve minutes from time Peter Osgood flung himself forward full length to head in Charlie Cooke's pass, and extra time brought Chelsea's most wonderful FA Cup moment of all as centre-half David Webb climbed to Hutch's long throw and headed the goal that brought the Cup to Stamford Bridge for the first time. No team had ever won the trophy after being behind three times in the Final, and for the fourth time in four ties since the war Chelsea had overcome Leeds.

But it is all too long since the Cup worked out right against Arsenal, who dismissed Chelsea in the semi-finals of 1950 and 1952 and in last season's quarter-final—on all three occasions after a replay. Peter Osgood's exquisite shot that opened the scoring in Chelsea's latest FA Cup-tie deserved to win any match. It was not to be, however, but it added to the magical FA Cup memories of Chelsea which we cherish as they attempt again in 1973–74 to redress the balance of only one success after nearly seventy years of endeavour in the greatest knockout tournament of all.

Chelsea's Greatest Goalscorers

SIX Chelsea stars have stood out above all others in the club's history for one particular talent—their ability to put the ball in the net. Each has scored more than a century of goals for Chelsea, and collectively their total exceeds eight hundred. Their names and the years of their wonderful scoring exploits for the Blues: George Hilsdon (1906–12), George Mills (1929–39), Roy Bentley (1948–56), Jimmy Greaves (1957–61), Bobby Tambling (1959–70), Peter Osgood (1964–73).

GEORGE HILSDON

WHAT is still Chelsea's record League score was achieved on the opening day of their second season, 1 September 1906. Glossop came to Stamford Bridge for a Second Division fixture and the new attraction for Chelsea fans was 19-year-old centre-forward, George Hilsdon, signed that summer from West Ham United. To make room for him, manager Jackie Robertson dropped Frank Pearson, who, only a few months earlier, had finished Chelsea's first season as top scorer with 18 League goals.

If that was a surprise, what followed was the first real goal-scoring sensation in Chelsea history, for Glossop were beaten 9–2 and Hilsdon scored five of them in a start that has never been equalled. A month later he was picked by the Football League against the Irish League in Belfast, and celebrated with a hat-trick in a 6–0 win.

Hilsdon was a chance discovery by Chelsea. During their first season, manager Robertson went to a Fulham–West Ham reserve match, specifically to watch a West Ham half-back who had been recommended. Instead he was struck by the young inside-left in the same side. Declared Robertson: 'He will make an ideal centre-forward—I'd like to see him start next season in a Chelsea shirt.' Which Hilsdon so spectacularly did, on a free transfer!

By the end of his first season Chelsea had played themselves into the First Division and Hilsdon made the biggest individual contribution, leading their scorers with 27 goals. The following season (1907–08) he wrote his name indelibly in the Chelsea records as a Cup marksman. In the first round of the FA Cup, Chelsea were drawn away to Worksop, but by mutual agreement the tie was switched to Stamford Bridge. As well as their share of the bigger gate, Worksop received a 9–1 thrashing. To this day, that remains Chelsea's biggest FA Cup score and the six Hilsdon netted is still the highest individual match total by a Chelsea player.

Those six goals helped to make Hilsdon the club's first scoring 'centurion', because his aggregate in League football totalled 98 in 150 games over six seasons as follows: 27 in 1906–7, 24 in 1907–8, 25 in 1908–9, 3 in 1909–10 (most of which he missed through injury), 18 in 1910–11 and 1 in 1911–12. Hilsdon was the complete centre-forward of his day. Strong on the ball, he had pace with skill, kept both wings well supplied and hit shots left foot and right with a speed that earned him the description 'Gatling Gun'. As well as goals, George collected caps while he was with Chelsea, playing in eight full internationals for England between 1907–9—three against Ireland and one apiece against Scotland, Wales, Austria, Hungary and Bohemia.

In season 1911–12 Hilsdon, London-born, returned to West Ham. He left behind at Stamford Bridge a lasting reminder of his skills in the form of a weather-vane mounted on top of the East Stand. The footballer model it depicted was George Hilsdon, a worthy figure to look down on Chelsea football for the next 60 years, until the stand was dismantled at the start of modern redevelopment in June 1972.

GEORGE MILLS

Another Londoner named George was the next player to complete a century of goals for Chelsea—George Mills in the 1930s. He became the first to reach three figures for the club exclusively in League football.

There is no scope at First Division level nowadays for part-time footballers, but that was what Mills was—after joining Chelsea, he continued to work for a London printing firm and did his football training in the evenings—and what a welcome Christmas gift he proved to Chelsea followers when he made his début in December 1929 within a few days of signing amateur for the club.

Above: George Hilsdon : Five goals in his first game for Chelsea on 1 September, 1906 is still the Football League record for any player on debut.

Below: The model of George Hilsdon that looked down on Chelsea football for more than 60 years until the old East Stand was demolished last year.

Above: George Mills, whose goalscoring for Chelsea through the 30's was halted by the war.

He came from Deptford and developed with Bromley to the point of being noticed by David Calderhead, whose managerial reign at Stamford Bridge from 1907–33 remains the longest on record.

Halfway through the 1929–30 season Chelsea were in the lower half of the Second Division table as a result of moderate form at home and less than that away. Something needed to be done, and in the first of the three Christmas fixtures, at home to Preston, a chance was taken with the 20-year-old 'unknown' George Mills at centre-forward.

Within two minutes of the start of his début he scored and Preston were beaten 5–0. Next, Blackpool were defeated 4–0 and a 1–1 draw in the return holiday fixture at Blackpool meant a five-point Christmas for Chelsea. Bringing speed, sharpshooting and dashing enthusiasm to the attack, Mills was at once a favourite with the Stamford Bridge crowd. Chelsea spent the rest of that season steadily climbing the Second Division and finally winning promotion as runners-up to Blackpool. Mills was top scorer with 14 goals in 20 games—a fine return from half a season's football.

During the next two seasons Mills found himself playing second fiddle to Scottish International, Hughie Gallacher. Then came the challenge of Ireland's Joe Bambrick, but George, a player with a big heart for his only League club, outstayed them both as the loyal understudy ever-ready to give his best when the call came. With 14 goals he did most to keep Chelsea up when relegation threatened in 1933–34.

His finest season was 1936–37 with 22 of Chelsea's 52 First Division goals in 32 appearances. With 13 goals he was again top scorer in 1937–38, when he won his three England caps—all of them in a winning side. His brief international career began spectacularly that October with three goals in a 5–1 victory over Ireland in Belfast. A month later Mills helped England beat Wales 2–1 at Middlesbrough and in December he played in the 5–4 defeat of Czechoslovakia at Tottenham. In those three internationals he had Chelsea goalkeeper, Vic Woodley, for company, but George was followed as England centre-forward next season by Everton's Tommy Lawton, who was also to succeed him as Chelsea's leader when League football was resumed in 1946 after the war.

Mills' first-class career was ended by the outbreak of war in 1939 on a total of 116 League goals in 220 appearances, mostly at centre-forward but occasionally inside. After leaving the game, George worked his way up to the position of sales director

Opposite: After he gave up playing, George Mills stayed ever-loyal to Chelsea. Here he is seen (extreme right) as 'team attendant' travelling everywhere with the 'A' side in 1955, and when Chelsea pulled out of the Metropolitan League George remained the keenest of Saturday afternoon supporters at Stamford Bridge.

with the London printing firm he served for 20 years. His hobby remained football—Chelsea football. For a time in the 1950s he travelled every week with the club's 'A' side, and when that was disbanded he spent his Saturdays supporting Chelsea with all the enthusiasm of his playing days. One of the great joys of his life was Chelsea's FA Cup success in April 1970, and only three months later Stamford Bridge was deeply saddened to learn that 'Gentleman George' had died suddenly while on holiday at Torquay, aged 62.

ROY BENTLEY

Captain of Chelsea in League Championship year (1954–55) and their leading scorer for eight consecutive seasons, Roy Bentley gave wonderful value for the £11,000 paid by manager, Billy Birrell, for his transfer from Newcastle in January 1948. He was bought to replace Tommy Lawton, who had moved to Notts County, and at first found difficulty in settling down in London. 'I almost felt like packing up,' recalls Roy, 'but knew I had got to fight my problems and justify myself.'

Chelsea fans certainly expected more than three goals from Bentley's first 14 League games to the end of that season. Fully fit for the start of 1948–49, he was a different player, scoring 20 First Division goals and setting a standard he was long to maintain as the club's top scorer.

Under Birrell, Bentley played a roving role. Ted Drake used him almost exclusively as a spearhead. In his 12 full internationals for England he played five times in the centre and seven times at inside-forward. He shot with power in the right foot and accuracy in the left, and on the Chelsea training ground spent many an hour developing his heading to a degree of sheer brilliance. Roy jumped with springs in his heels. With perfect timing, he regularly climbed above taller opponents and had the knack of 'hanging' in the air before heading the ball past despairing goalkeepers.

Almost regularly at the start of the Fifties, Bentley's goals kept Chelsea narrowly clear of relegation. In the FA Cup semi-final against Arsenal at Tottenham in 1950, he gave Chelsea a magnificent two-goal lead, but it was not enough to take the club to Wembley. If that was the biggest disappointment of his days at Stamford Bridge, his greatest delight was to lead Chelsea to the League Championship in 1955—a distinction known to no Chelsea captain before or since.

Having seen the club through many relegation storms, he

Roy Bentley—Chelsea's Championship-winning captain. What power in that right foot!

Roy Bentley came from Newcastle to succeed Tommy Lawton. He did so with wonderful headers like this.

could appreciate the Championship sunshine, and when Chelsea went to the top of the table towards the end of March, Roy declared: 'We're there for the rest of the season.' That promise was fulfilled. His own contribution was 21 goals in 41 League appearances. In a 4–3 win at home to Newcastle, his old team, in January, Bentley scored his first Chelsea hat-trick to celebrate seven years with the club; his other three-goal performance that season was in England's 3–2 victory against Wales at Wembley.

Born at Bristol, Roy Bentley went into Rovers' office from school but turned professional with Bristol City. After serving in the Royal Navy, he returned to Ashton Gate, then moved to Newcastle. His best was still to come—with Chelsea.

Bentley obtained his 100th League goal for Chelsea against West Bromwich in October 1954. With a career aggregate of 128 goals in 324 matches he took over from George Mills as the club's record League marksman, and if there were comparatively few more to come with Fulham, who turned him into a centre-half, there was nevertheless still a lot of football in Roy Bentley when, in September 1956 he moved from Stamford Bridge to Craven Cottage.

JIMMY GREAVES

Now the 33-year-old executive director of a packing-case company, travel agencies and sports goods shops, Jimmy Greaves is as prosperous in business as ever he was in football . . . which is saying something. He wasn't just a goalscorer. He was a goal machine, a genius brought to the game from Chelsea's nursery who achieved the astonishing striking rate of 124 First Division goals in 157 matches and only four seasons before Stamford Bridge lost him to the lure of Italian football.

Greaves was born at Ilford on 20 February 1940, and began his scoring feats at Kingswood School, Dagenham. Jimmy Thompson, then Chelsea's chief scout, spotted him as a 12-year-old and when, three years later, he brought the boy prodigy to Stamford Bridge, he introduced him to manager, Ted Drake, with the words: 'Meet the Champ!' And when Greaves became a professional on 13 May 1957, Drake sent Thompson along with the papers saying, 'You found him—you deserve to sign him. The credit is yours.'

In the previous season junior Jimmy surpassed anything ever achieved for Chelsea by scoring 114 goals in all matches, and was presented with an illuminated address to mark the feat. On 24 August 1957, the first day of the new season, he was launched in League football, away to Tottenham, and scored in a 1–1 draw. 'Of all the goals I got, that one will always stick in my mind for the reception the Chelsea fans gave me,' says Jimmy.

Slightly built at 5 ft. 8 in. and just over 10 st., Greaves cut First Division defences to pieces with devastating runs, often from halfway, that combined supreme ball control, high-speed dribbling, stealth and courage, and an ice-cold brain. Sharp as a needle, slippery as an eel and the surest of shots was our Jim.

Three times he scored five in a match for Chelsea—at home to Wolves (6–2) in 1958–59, away to Preston (5–4) in 1959–60 and at home to West Bromwich Albion (7–1) in 1960–61). Season by season his League totals were: 1957–58—22 goals in

Above: Jimmy Greaves, goalscoring genius for Chelsea from 1957–61.

Opposite: Jimmy Greaves leaving Tottenham's defence in chaos on the day he made his League debut—with a goal, of course!

35 games; 1958–59—32 goals in 42 games; 1959–60—29 goals in 40 games; and 1960–61—41 goals in 40 games. While with Chelsea Jimmy played 11 of his 12 Under-23 Internationals and won the first 15 of his 57 full England caps.

With a hat-trick at home to Manchester City (6–3) on 19 November 1960, Greaves became the first player in soccer history to complete 100 goals before the age of 21. His farewell match at Stamford Bridge, before his £80,000 transfer to AC Milan, was against Nottingham Forest on 29 April 1961. Chelsea won 4–3 and, typically, the little wonderman scored all four goals.

Modern trends make it probable that Greaves's 41 First Division goals that season will long remain a Chelsea record. Now retired from the game, Jimmy can give his views on football past, present and future from a detached position, and what he has to say is not very good news for strikers just arriving on the scene: 'I cannot see any newcomer scoring 124 League goals in four seasons as I did for Chelsea. That is not to say today's players lack talent. It is the law of the day. Winning something has become so important to clubs that everything is geared to defence nowadays. As a result, two or three forwards are having to do the work that used to be done by five, so there have got to be fewer goals.

'Were my own scoring exploits in any way responsible for the situation today? I don't want to claim any responsibility for the present goal shortage. All I can say is that, in my early days, everyone wanted to score goals, and a lot more matches would end 4–3 or 3–2 instead of 1–0 as they so often do now.

'I am convinced, though, that if Denis Law and I were at our peak today we would still score more than most. I'm equally sure that over our careers we would not collect as many as we did. I think it will still be possible for a player just coming into the game to get 100 goals for one club—but he must be prepared to take a very long time doing it.'

BOBBY TAMBLING

Between his League début at home to West Ham on 7 February 1959 and his final appearance away to West Bromwich on Easter Monday, 30 March 1970, Bobby Tambling achieved the all-time Chelsea scoring record of 202 goals in 370 competitive first-team matches. They comprised 164 League goals, 25 in the FA Cup, 10 in the League Cup—all records for the club—plus three in the Fairs Cup, and when Tambling returned to Stamford Bridge as a Crystal Palace player on Easter Saturday 1971, his feats as a Chelsea marksman were put on permanent record with the presentation of an illuminated address by chairman, Brian Mears.

Like Hilsdon, Mills and Greaves before him, Tambling scored on his Chelsea début. In that 3–2 win against West Ham he played outside-left and was partnered by Greaves . . . and when Jimmy left for Italy two years later the mantle of Chelsea goalscorer-in-chief fell on Bobby Tambling.

'Sorry as I was to see Jimmy go, his departure gave me an earlier chance to establish myself. I had picked up a lot from him, but knew it was no good trying to set myself up as "another Jimmy Greaves". I had to pursue my own style,' reflects Bobby, who was to head Chelsea's list of League scorers in five of the next eight seasons.

At the end of their first winter without Greaves, Chelsea were relegated, despite the emergence of a new double-spearhead in Tambling (20 goals) and Barry Bridges (19). A year later Bobby captained Chelsea back to the First Division as top scorer with 35 goals, his best haul in any season. Four of them came in the final match in which Portsmouth were beaten 7–0 at Stamford Bridge, and Tambling led the team into the directors' box to take their bow.

Left foot shots struck powerfully on the run were Bobby's speciality. On two other occasions he scored four in a match—at Charlton in December 1962 and away to Arsenal in March 1964—but his peak solo performance was five Chelsea goals in a 6–2 victory away to Aston Villa in September 1966.

44 Bobby Tambling, the all-time record scorer for Chelsea with a total of 202 goals.

The left foot brought most of Bobby Tambling's goals. Here, in a 2–2 draw at Leeds in January 1965, his shot beats Sprake but hits the post. George Graham (No. 8) snapped up the rebound.

During his time with Chelsea, Bobby earned three full England caps (1 goal) and made 13 Under-23 appearances (11 goals). He contributed six goals to the club's League Cup success in season 1964–65 and six in the 1966–67 FA Cup campaign, including Chelsea's lone reply to Tottenham's two in the final at Wembley.

Again, like Greaves, Tambling was discovered as a schoolboy by Jimmy Thompson. He travelled from his home at Havant, near Portsmouth, to join Chelsea as a 15-year-old junior in July 1957. He signed professional in September 1958 and in the final against Preston got a hat-trick in the FA Youth Cup-winning side of 1960.

Bobby reached his century of League goals, in 177 appearances, away to West Ham in November 1965. A penalty against Spurs at Stamford Bridge in October 1966 brought him his 151st first-team goal, beating the Chelsea record previously held by Roy Bentley. With the winner at home to Coventry in March 1969, he passed another milestone—his 200th goal for the club.

At the age of 27, Tambling was rewarded with a £6,000 Testimonial in that 1968–69 season. In his special match, Charlton were beaten 5–1 but, ironically, Chelsea's record sharp-shooter did not get his name on the scoresheet that night. Bobby spent much of the following season fighting a knee injury. In January 1970 he joined Crystal Palace on a month's loan; at home to Stoke in March he made his 300th League appearance for Chelsea; and three months later he moved permanently to Selhurst Park.

PETER OSGOOD

And so to the sixth player to complete a century of first-team goals in the service of Chelsea—Ossie. On an occasion of many scoring records, he reached his hundred (in 258 matches spread over eight seasons) when he shot the first in the 13–0 win in the European Cup-Winners' Cup first round second leg at home to Jeunesse Hautcharage, of Luxembourg, on 29 September 1971. By the end of the night he had joined Hilsdon, Greaves and Tambling on the list of players who have scored five in a match for Chelsea and, having got three in the first leg (8–0) in Luxembourg, he equalled the European individual record of eight in a home-and-away tie.

From the time of his début, on which he was twice a scorer in the League Cup at home to Workington in December 1964, Peter Osgood brought a new term to Chelsea football, the 'Osgoal'. His was a rapid arrival on the scene, for Tommy Docherty had made him a professional only three months earlier and within six months of signing him on amateur forms from local league football at Windsor.

Greaves apart, Osgood has brought greater individual flair to Chelsea forward play than anyone in the club's history. In an era of ever-tightening defences, he has proved the 'big occasion' man, and of all his club goals the three most important were his diving header that equalised in the FA Cup Final replay against Leeds at Old Trafford in April 1970 and, in Athens a year later, his shot that gave Chelsea the lead in the Cup-Winners' Cup Final against Real Madrid, followed two nights later by the replay winner. Last season's spectacular volley in the FA Cup sixth round at home to Arsenal provided further evidence of the heights to which Cup football can raise Ossie's game.

A broken right leg sustained in the League Cup at Blackpool in October 1966 kept Osgood out of that season's FA Cup Final.

'The wizard of Os.'

When Chelsea got there again in 1969–70, he scored in every round, including the final replay, for a season's total of 31 goals, which he equalled in 1971–72. He earned three England caps in 1969–70, away to Belgium and as substitute against Rumania and Czechoslovakia in the Mexico World Cup.

By the end of last season Peter had taken his first-team goal total for Chelsea to 140 in 347 matches. To what extent does he consider the striker's role has changed during his nine years in the first-class game? 'We are losing out in today's defensive brand of football. There is an 11th Commandment—Thou Shalt Not Score—set by top sides like Arsenal and Leeds, and and even less skilful teams have learned to defend tightly.

'Three seasons ago Ian Hutchinson and I were going great. Between us we knocked in 53 of Chelsea's 99 goals. If we missed a chance, we didn't worry too much because we could reckon on another one coming along soon. But now I do worry if I miss one, because it might be my only opportunity of the game. Not so long ago I could count on getting anything up to 15 goals in a season from close range. Not any more. Everything is so tight at the back, and strikers are finding themselves increasingly outnumbered. For half a game at West Bromwich last season I played centre-half. Compared with playing up front, I found it easy. If I can keep going that long, I might take it up permanently when I'm about forty!'

Opposite: Goalkeepers don't stop shots like this from Peter Osgood—only the net can do that.

British Football Still Best

says a Chelsea star of the 1947-57 era—
KEN ARMSTRONG

HOME, to me, is three places: Bradford, where I was born and bred; Chelsea, where I played all my football from the time I came out of the Army in December 1946 and signed for Billy Birrell until my farewell game in May 1957; and New Zealand, the country to which the Armstrong family emigrated when I retired.

After 15 years away from the game at First Division level, I returned last November wondering how I would find the British soccer scene. I was agreeably surprised to see Stamford Bridge half-demolished—if only the place had been rebuilt years ago! —and my reaction to the game generally, after a four and a half weeks' stay in the UK, was: 'Great stuff, this modern soccer. Don't let anyone kid you otherwise'.

And, with one proviso, all the ingredients are there for something even greater to come. Better overall performers, modern equipment (I wish we'd had waterproofed footballs, among other things, when I was playing), terrific training facilities, good referees—yes, I mean that—and an increasing amount of covered accommodation for supporters. What more could one ask for?

That's all on the credit side. But, and it's a very big but, I was all too aware that something is in danger of killing the game. That is the over-cautious 'keep a point at all costs' approach by managers and coaches. While I was here last winter I watched eight League games in England and Scotland and had numerous discussions with those who hold the reins in professional football. Very much in evidence was a 'safety first and avoid relegation' attitude. Too many sides adopt a 4–4–2 formation merely to hang on to a point, and only when they are a goal behind with time running out do they put some attacking urgency into their play. I saw Leeds United, away to Arsenal, quite content to hold on to a penalty goal lead until goalkeeping

Ken Armstrong in typically determined action for the Blues. Chelsea have never had a more wholehearted or enthusiastic player.

30 May, 1957—the day the Armstrongs emigrated to New Zealand. Ken and family leave Waterloo for Southampton to board the liner 'Southern Cross,' with his wife Betty holding $2\frac{1}{2}$-year-old Shirley and the boys at the carriage window (left to right) Ronnie, 5, Brian, 8, and Michael, 10.

errors put them behind. Only then did they push up on attack with any purpose in their play.

Not all the blame can be levelled at the team manager, coach or whatever title he holds as the man in charge. For example, there is something radically wrong with today's thinking when some clubs award manager, coach and players a bonus *for avoiding relegation*. How's that for a negative approach! No wonder attacking ideas are limited. To me, as a football man who still eats, drinks and sleeps soccer and with three sons playing, that sort of attitude is nothing short of criminal.

In season 1954–55 when Chelsea won the Championship, with more than a million fans attending the home League matches at an average of just over 48,000, the one bad aspect of our play was the emphasis on the long through ball *even when it was not on*. Then we saw the emergence of the short pass, the 'keep possession, go back' type of play of the Continentals.

Some folk liked it because it looked different and more skilful but, believe me, the hard, rugged, physical goalscoring game of the British, however bad, had more to offer than a poor Continental game. Keeping possession can be very boring from the sideline and, present day, it is being overdone in my opinion.

Players are no longer looking for the through ball or the priority pass, as I call it. They are too conditioned to the square and back ball. There is all too seldom the quick counter-attack when a defender dispossesses an opposing forward. Instead of a penetrating pass and the quick follow-up, he invariably works overtime on the ball, turns back, fiddles again and gives the easy ball back to a rear defender or the goalkeeper. And at that stage *the game is dead*. They used to say attack was the best form of defence, but now the word 'attack' is substituted by 'possession'. Oh, for a manager who would take a calculated risk and go out to win away matches instead of playing, as so many do, not to lose them.

I have read much about falling gates in Britain and various reasons have been advanced—not enough goals, over-defensive formations, too much television, etc. I would add 'action replays allied to over-exposure of the game on TV'. These replays are terrific . . . something you don't get in the flesh on

Left: It was like old times to see Ken Armstrong in the Chelsea dressing-room last winter, when he was a welcome visitor from New Zealand.

Right: 'Now that I'm here, I'd like to study a full training session and see how it compares with my playing days,' says Ken to Dave Sexton, while John Hollins gets on with some ball practice.

'We didn't do "doggies" in the 1950's,' observes Ken (above, right of Dave Sexton) as Ian Hutchinson sprints against the stop-watch.

Saturday afternoon. Television not only provides an immediate replay of goals. It shows movement leading up to a near-miss. It shows controversial decisions like penalties, sending-off incidents, and in one game I saw the action replay of a particular foul at least four times, enough to settle doubts in anyone's mind . . . and enough to put the referee on trial. Unfairly so.

Since 1957 I have been 12,000 miles away from big-time football and as yet I'm not conditioned to soccer on television. It's great. But, as I see it, they do it too well! Why bother about going to a match when something even better is supplied on TV? No doubt the square box won't deter the loyal team supporters on a wet, miserable Saturday afternoon, but the missing masses are the lukewarm, non-fanatical fellows who used to enjoy mingling with the crowd for their Saturday afternoon entertainment. Now they can get their full share from TV at no cost and in armchair comfort.

Perhaps it's the female soccer population that is 'missing'. I imagine probably more women go to football now than ever before, but it's still a comparatively small percentage. One reason could be the foul language one hears flowing even from the stand seats nowadays, as my wife and I heard at a First Division match last December. Incidentally, it will be interesting to see how Chelsea's female support grows as the new stadium, with all its modern amenities, takes shape.

What about referees? Those I saw at First Division level last season did an excellent job. They have a lot to put up with, especially from some so-called stars who use their mouths more than their heads. My one big criticism is not of referees but of the system which requires them to take names for 'intent'. It's no longer enough to do the normal refereeing job; you need to be a mind-reader as well.

If referees are obliged to take names for over-enthusiastic tackles, as I noticed last season here, then soon football will not be worth watching or playing. I was left wondering how silly the game can get by an incident when I watched Leeds at home to West Ham. Bobby Moore flung himself sideways to chest a ball, but his timing was slightly 'off' and he handled. I was astonished to hear the crowd roaring for his name to be taken. Yes, there is room for a good deal of commonsense application all round, from legislators, referees, managers, coaches, players . . . and fans. Given that, this greatest of games will become greater still.

'And we didn't have such a good training ground as Mitcham in my time.' Below: Left to right, Tommy Baldwin, Ian Hutchinson, Ken Armstrong and Dave Sexton.

Some straightforward conclusions:

1. Soccer needs managers with attacking ideas who can coach for penetration.

2. The game would benefit from less television—especially those controversial action replays.

3. Referees. Don't be too hasty in taking a player's name for a foul—you are in danger of choking the game to death.

4. Managers: Persuade Authority to allow your captain to approach the referee . . . and discipline other players who shout their mouths off.

To finish on a Chelsea note, my best wishes, as always, for the Blues this season. And already I look forward to my next trip here from New Zealand—possibly next year, when I hope to be visiting Europe again for the World Cup in West Germany—because, like all Chelsea fans, I am so eager to see Stamford Bridge changing from an out-of-date football ground to a stadium of the future.

One special request to groundsman George Anstiss and his staff. When it comes to shifting the pitch (I understand it is being sited some yards nearer the West Stand as well as moving slightly North), I hope you'll be able to get it flattened out. For as long as I've known Stamford Bridge, there as been a 'crown' on the ground, running from goal to goal right down the pitch, and over the years it must have prevented a lot of Chelsea goals. I know a football pitch is the same for both teams, but for years Chelsea have faced this 'crown problem' in every home game.

I was reminded of it when I watched the match against Crystal Palace last November. At the North end Alan Hudson closed in from the right for a shot on the run and connected just as he reached the 'hump'. Watch this one rise, I told myself. It did—like an aircraft climbing off a runway. We shall never know how many points that 'crown' has cost Chelsea, but it could be a sizeable clue to the club's consistent failure to do as well as they ought here at The Bridge.

Albert Sewell writes:

Chelsea fans whose support goes back sixteen years or more remember Ken Armstrong as one of the finest, most enthusiastic and wholehearted players ever to serve the club. A bank clerk in his native Bradford before call-up, he became a product of Army football, and from the time of his first appearance, in the opening League match of 1947-48, it was apparent that Chelsea had acquired a player of outstanding quality. He cost

Above: Together again, 25 years after they were First Division team-mates for Chelsea in season 1947–48: Trainer Harry Medhurst, Ken, and Dick Spence, now Youth team trainer.

Below: The way he used to do it! Back to Chelsea's 1954–55 Championship-winning season, Ken Armstrong (left) heading the eighth goal . . . result Chelsea 5, Manchester United 6.

Life is good in New Zealand, and outside working hours and football coaching Ken finds time for golf, swimming, barbecuing, hiking . . . and horse-riding.

the club a £10 signing fee; £150,000 would not buy his like today.

In his first season he distinguished himself for a time in the unenviable role of centre-forward successor to Tommy Lawton, but right-half was the position in which he was to star consistently for ten seasons. Armstrong was a member of what is still the only Chelsea side to win the League Championship (1954–55), and at Wembley that April helped England inflict what was then the heaviest defeat (7–2) Scotland had ever suffered in the International tournament. But for Billy Wright's near permanent claim to the No. 4 shirt in the first eight seasons after the war, he must have won more than that one England cap.

In January 1956, on a Cup trip to Hartlepool, Ken went down with a severe chill. After turning out at home to Sunderland the following week, he developed pleurisy and did not play again that season. He captained Chelsea for much of the following winter and then, in May 1957, he decided the time had come for him to retire and seek a new life with his family in

Opposite: The Armstrong family home in Auckland, New Zealand. In more ways than one he has travelled far, has the lad who was born at Bradford and educated, football-wise, at Chelsea.

New Zealand, where the climate is more friendly to those who have been affected by chest trouble.

Ken Armstrong took with him the distinction of having played 362 League games (24 goals), a Chelsea record subsequently exceeded by Peter Bonetti and Ron Harris. Our loss was certainly New Zealand's gain, for as an NZ soccer selector and coach to the Mount Wellington club in Auckland he has done much to raise playing standards in his adopted country.

Sons Brian (24) and Ronnie (21) both play National League football for Mount Wellington. The third and eldest son, Michael (26), a radio and TV technician in Salisbury, Rhodesia, has a daughter, and at 49 Ken is the youngest-looking grandfather you're ever likely to meet. Daughter Shirley, 18, lives at home with Ken and his Scottish wife, Betty, in Auckland. A luxury home it is too, that Ken has built himself . . . and a luxury life the Armstrongs lead in New Zealand's agreeable climate. Always a keen golfer in his Chelsea days, Ken gets in at least one full day's play each week, besides family hiking, horse-riding and frequent trips to the nearby beach. Every day is still a new adventure to him, just as every match was throughout his playing career.

Ken's trip to Britain last season was a triple mission—part business (he visited the head office in London of his company in New Zealand, The Colonial Mutual Life Assurance Society Ltd.), part holiday and, on behalf of New Zealand football, a tour study of big-club training methods in England and Scotland.

He was particularly impressed by the extensive practice Chelsea put in at 'bending' the ball from free-kicks. And, as well as tactical ideas, he took home a lot of new kit for his Mount Wellington team.

Stranger Than Fiction

WHEN the present rebuilding programme is complete, Chelsea hope their enterprise in constructing a virtually new stadium will be rewarded by Stamford Bridge becoming the venue for some of the big fixtures on the football calendar. Who knows . . . the FA Cup Final itself might one day be staged here again? What an occasion that would be, especially if Chelsea played in the final on their own ground!

It very nearly happened once before, in 1920—the first of three years the FA Cup Final took place at Stamford Bridge before Wembley Stadium opened in 1923. Chelsea had reached the last final (1915) before the competition was abandoned during the 1914–18 War, and when it was resumed in season 1919–20 Stamford Bridge was named well in advance as the venue for the final. With wins against Bolton, Swindon, Leicester City and Bradford, Chelsea played their way into the semi-finals and, with arrangements too far advanced to be altered, the FA Council chamber was full of red faces at the prospect of a club playing at home in the final. But the situation was averted by the semi-final at Bramall Lane, Sheffield, where the result was Chelsea 1, Aston Villa 3.

* * * * *

During Tommy Docherty's six seasons as their manager, Chelsea were concerned in some extraordinary transfers, none more remarkable than those involving Alex Stepney. In May 1966 Docherty paid Millwall £50,000, then the record goalkeeper fee, for Stepney. Only four months later Docherty transferred him to Manchester United—fee again £50,000. Stepney moved North ten days after making his only League appearance for Chelsea in a 3–0 win at Southampton on 3 September.

Until 1955 Chelsea had never earned any honours. Then, in their Golden Jubilee year, it all happened—every Chelsea team won a prize. Left to right: Metropolitan League Challenge Cup ('A' team); South-East Counties League Championship Cup (Juniors); Football League Championship Cup; Metropolitan League Professional Cup; Football Combination League Cup (Reserves).

It could only happen to Chelsea! They are the only club in FA Cup history to lose three matches in the competition *in the same season*. How come? It happened in season 1945–46, when, to avoid travel by large numbers of spectators directly after the war, the Cup was run on a two-leg basis. In the fourth round Chelsea beat West Ham United 2–0 at Stamford Bridge and lost the return match 0–1 at Upton Park, so winning the tie 2–1 on aggregate. Then, in round five, they met Aston Villa, losing 0–1 at home and by the same score at Villa Park.

Over the years Chelsea have been renowned for classic come-backs in matches that appeared lost, but it is doubtful if they will ever exceed the powers of recovery they showed in a First Division match at Blackpool on 24 October 1970. The half-time score was Blackpool 3, Chelsea 0, at which stage 19-year-old goalkeeper John Phillips was looking decidedly down in the mouth on his First Division début, although no blame for the situation could be attached to him. With 20 minutes left and no change in the score, manager Dave Sexton decided the time had come to make a switch. He took off Tommy Baldwin, substituted Charlie Cooke, moved Peter Houseman to left-back and sent David Webb up front . . . and instantly everything clicked. Keith Weller shot Chelsea's first goal from the edge of the box (71 mins.), Webb headed the second (77 mins.) and three minutes later Weller drove in the equaliser after Peter Osgood won the ball from Blackpool 'keeper Thomson. The high point of the drama was still to come, because in the last minute Weller centred hard into the goalmouth and Blackpool defender Dave Hatton kicked the ball into his own net. It gave Chelsea a 4–3 victory they still couldn't believe until they bought the London papers after flying back from the game that Saturday night.

* * * * *

Chelsea went until the last week of last season before being awarded a first-team penalty. If they had been given one earlier, Peter Bonetti or John Phillips would not have taken it, but 50-odd years ago Chelsea did have a penalty-taking goalkeeper, by name Benjamin Howard Baker, one of the truly great amateurs of his day. The First Division match summary in *Lloyd's Sunday News* dated 20 November 1921 read: Chelsea 1 (Howard Baker), Bradford City 0 (35,000). Above it ran the headline: *GOALKEEPER'S GOAL GIVES CHELSEA WIN*. And this was how the match report colourfully described the scene:

'Chelsea have found a player who can score, and his name is B. Howard Baker and he is a goalkeeper. Two minutes from the end at Stamford Bridge yesterday, the amateur left his goal, cantered leisurely up the field and, twelve yards from goal, sent a low, well-placed shot past Ewart into the net. It was a shot taken from the penalty spot, I had better add.

'Few games can ever have had such a dramatic climax. Bradford City, with one player cooling his temper in the dressing-room and Hibbert a limping passenger at outside-right, had survived all sorts of adventures and had every reason to believe they had won the point. Suddenly Cock broke clear and was dribbling into a shooting position when Watson, Bradford's left-back, palpably handled. A staccato appeal, and the referee pointed to the penalty spot. Not since Willis Rippon scored an equalising goal with a last-minute penalty in a Cup semi-final for Bristol City on this same ground has there been such excitement at Stamford Bridge.

'Harrow, haunted by memories of two bungled penalty attempts this season, declined to trust himself with a kick upon which the result turned. The feeble shooting of the Chelsea forwards all afternoon made his choice the more difficult. Then he had an inspiration. He called up Howard Baker from the Chelsea goal. Baker, who had been making signs indicative of his anxiety to try his luck, went joyfully up the field and, probably the coolest man present, drove the ball at express pace well and truly home past Ewart's right hand. All that was left of the gate cheered hoarsely.

'The amateur, in his meteoric career in a Chelsea uniform, has now saved a penalty and scored from one at Stamford Bridge. Not since Tiny Joyce used to perform this office for Millwall has a London crowd had such a novelty.'

That happened during the first of Howard Baker's five seasons with Chelsea, but it was the only time his name appeared on the club scoresheet. A game or two later, against Arsenal at Highbury, he tried again from the penalty spot. This time it did not come off. Williamson, the Arsenal goalkeeper, made a brilliant save and Chelsea lost 1–0. Whereupon, the risks of a goalkeeper failing to score with a penalty-kick having been demonstrated, Howard Baker was relieved of the job. But this fine amateur 'keeper with a yearning for the unusual (he had University honours in various sports, including the high-jump record; sent the Chelsea crowd into choruses of 'Oohs' and 'Aahs' as he dashed beyond the penalty-area to save or kicked prodigious clearances the length of the field for the other goalkeeper to deal with) was never really happy to see some other Chelsea player taking a penalty-kick.

* * * * *

Wearing red shirts last season when required to change from their regular blue was different for Chelsea, but not exactly new. Did you know they have been Cup-winners at Wembley while wearing red? The occasion was the war-time Football League South Cup Final against Millwall on 7 April 1945. Because of a colour clash, both sides changed, with Chelsea in red shirts and white shorts and Millwall in white shirts and black shorts. After a 2–0 win, John Harris received the Cup from King George VI and is still the only captain to lead Chelsea to victory at Wembley.

* * * * *

At the end of season 1950–51 Chelsea survived one of the most remarkable relegation escapes in Football League history. With only four matches to play, this was how hopeless their position looked at the foot of the table (especially as they had not won for 14 games—five drawn, nine lost):

	P	W	D	L	F	A	Pts.
Everton	39	11	8	20	46	78	30
Sheffield Wed.	39	10	8	21	55	81	28
Chelsea	38	8	8	22	44	63	24

Even if Chelsea won those last four fixtures, they would total 32 points. But those who believed things could only get better were right. Three of the remaining matches were at home, and in the first of them Liverpool were beaten 1–0 by Bobby Smith's late goal. Next, Wolves came to Stamford Bridge and went into a fifth-minute lead, but the luckiest of penalties by Roy Bentley (after Bobby Smith tumbled in the area with no opponent within yards) brought Chelsea level, and they won 2–1 by Ken Armstrong's goal which was allowed even though he knocked down a bouncing ball with his hand on the way through.

The last-but-one fixture took Chelsea 'next door' to Fulham and there they again came from behind to win 2–1, Armstrong scoring both in reply to Bedford Jezzard's shock opener. So to 5 May, the last day of the season, with Chelsea at home to Bolton Wanderers while, by the greatest stroke of fortune, the other two threatened clubs, Sheffield Wednesday and Everton, clashed at Hillsborough.

At the Bridge nearly 40,000 saw Bentley jump twice to head Chelsea into a 2–0 lead. Bobby Smith made it three before half-time and, soon after, increased the margin to 4–0. Meanwhile, Sheffield Wednesday were beating Everton 6–0, so that all three clubs finally totalled 32 points, with Chelsea's goal average best by .044, or 1/25 of a goal. This was the outcome of one of football's most dramatic photo-finishes, with wins, draws and losses identical for each club:

	P	W	D	L	F	A.	Pts.	Goal Av.
Chelsea	42	12	8	22	53	65	32	.815
Sheffield Wed.	42	12	8	22	64	83	32	·771
Everton	42	12	8	22	48	86	32	·558

* * * * *

Since the last war, the fewest Football League matches played by any club between winning an FA Cup semi-final and appearing in the final is two by Chelsea in season 1966–67. The semi-final, in which they beat Leeds 1–0 at Villa Park, was as late as 29 April, and Chelsea were left with only two League fixtures to play (Leeds at home, 6 May, and Leicester away, 9 May) before meeting Tottenham at Wembley on 20 May.

* * * * *

Stamford Bridge is fast approaching its centenary as a sports venue. The stadium was formally declared open in April 1877 by the then Lord Mayor of London, one year after its lease came into the possession of the London Athletic Club. Originally the site was a market garden, and the railway line which still passes the ground on the East side (behind the newly-constructed stand) was laid on the bed of a tributary of the Thames. The British Amateur Athletic Championship was held here every year from 1877–1903, when the lease expired and the land was put up for sale. The purchaser was Henry Augustus Mears, one of London's largest contractors, and in his desire to see Stamford Bridge among the finest sports grounds in Britain, he laid out the football pitch, encircled by a cycling and running track, and accommodation for more than 80,000 people. Soon after coming into possession of the ground, Mr. Mears initiated the formation of Chelsea Football Club, which was registered in April 1905 with a capital of £5,000.

Autograph Gallery

Dave Sexton	Brian Bason
Peter Bonetti	John Boyle

Autograph Gallery

John Dempsey
Chris Garland

Mick Droy
Bill Garner

Autograph Gallery

Ron Harris
John Hollins

Marvin Hinton
Peter Houseman

Autograph Gallery

Alan Hudson
Steve Kember

Ian Hutchinson
Gary Locke

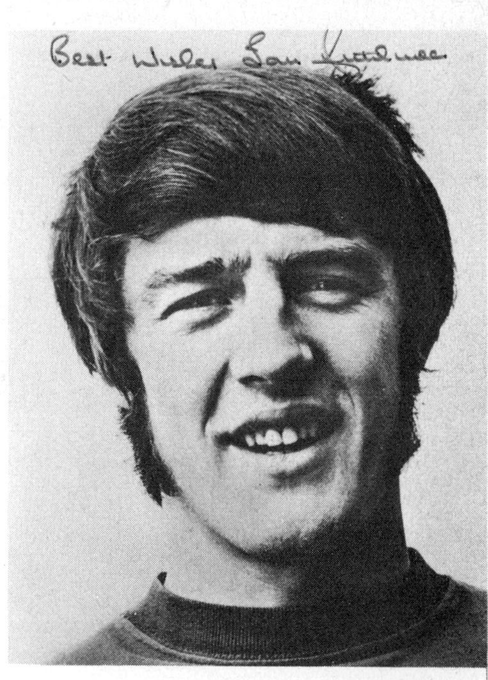

Autograph Gallery

Eddie McCreadie　　Peter Osgood
John Phillips　　David Webb

Chelsea Football Club was founded in March 1905, registered in April, elected to the Football League in May and kicked off in the Second Division, away to Stockport County, the following September. How was it launched on such a sudden rise to fame? Who were the players so swiftly brought together, the first to wear the Chelsea colours—then light blue shirts, white shorts? What were the hopes and prospects of the newest London club with the biggest ground in the capital? We return to the Stamford Bridge scene of 68 years ago, and see how the Club's beginning and future were viewed in November 1905 by their first manager in *The Book of Football,* a twelve-part publication, price sixpence.

The First Chelsea Team of all

by the first Chelsea manager—
JOHN TAIT ROBERTSON

In the whole long history of football, no club has rushed into fame with such sensational suddenness as Chelsea. In 1904 they did not exist. Now everyone interested in the game has heard of their splendid ground, their fine eleven and the great chance the club has of getting into the League proper (First Division) at the first time of asking.

Chelsea have come in on a huge tidal wave of popularity. The game is booming as it never boomed before. London is now as enthusiastic as Birmingham, Manchester, Liverpool or Glasgow, and it is the opinion of all the experts that the greatest of all cities will soon be the headquarters of the greatest of all winter games. I may be biased, but I believe, and a large number of men who have had a vast experience of the game think with me, that Chelsea is destined to be the leading club of the metropolis.

How this great football enterprise came to be launched is an interesting story. Some eight years ago Mr. H. A. Mears, a son of the late Mr. Joseph Mears, the well-known contractor, conceived the idea of turning the Stamford Bridge Athletic Ground into a football arena. He and his brother, Mr. J. T. Mears, have played football all their lives and, being as fond of

John Tait Robertson.

'Chelsea's manager was born at Dumbarton in 1877. His height is 5ft. 8in., and he weighs 11st. 6lb. Chelsea secured him from the Glasgow Rangers, and the success of the team under his able management is an eloquent testimony to his ability as an organiser. Mr. Robertson has played for Greenock Morton, Everton, Southampton and Glasgow Rangers. He is a famous International, having received no less than sixteen caps for Scotland, and has represented the Scottish League on seven occasions. Plays left half-back for Chelsea, is as keen a footballer as ever, despite the cares of management. He is married.'

sport as they were wealthy, determined to buy the piece of ground that seemed to them so eminently suited to their purpose.

It was more centrally situated than any other existing ground and large enough, when treated by a skilled architect, to hold the biggest crowd the most ambitious club manager ever dreamed of. Difficulties had to be overcome. A Mr. Stunt was the freeholder of the property, and a clause in the lease laid down that the London Athletic Club should be leaseholders until two years after the death of this gentleman. He lived until 1902, which gave the Athletic Club a long run. Directly it was possible, Mr. Mears bought the ground, having some four years previously secured the adjoining property. The Chelsea Club, with its present influential directorate and distinguished patrons, was then formed.

Last April I was engaged as manager. I was at that time a member of the Glasgow Rangers. We set to work at once on the engrossing and intensely difficult task of marshalling a strong side. Meanwhile, work had been proceeding apace on the new ground. Mr. Mears said he was prepared to spend £100,000 in order that our enclosure might be perfect in every detail; when the whole of the plans are completely carried out, it will fulfil this exacting description. The great grandstand is 120 yards long; the roof is suspended on great iron columns 70 feet from the ground and will accommodate 5,000 people.

The ground itself, when complete, will hold close upon 100,000 spectators, each of whom may enjoy an uninterrupted view of the game. When the roof, which is to be erected over the at-present unprotected side of the ground, is finished 50,000 enthusiasts will be enabled to watch Chelsea pulverise their opponents well sheltered from bad weather. It is hoped that some day the F.A. Cup Final will be played on the Chelsea ground. Already it is regarded as London's leading sports arena.

The London Athletic Club continue to hold their sports on the new cinder-track, and a short time ago 10,000 lovers of the Rugby game gathered to see Middlesex play the New Zealanders. That the League authorities are impressed by the enclosure is proved by the fact that they have arranged for the match between the English and Scottish Leagues to be played at Chelsea in March 1906.

But in football, as in war, the crux of the matter is the men. The best ground in the world would serve little purpose without an efficient eleven. So far, the players we have engaged have more than fulfilled expectations. The captain is Foulke. He is already one of the most popular players in London. When people first come to Chelsea they fall to admiring the proportions of the ground, then the proportions of Foulke, and next his unquestionable skill as a goalkeeper. He weighs 22st. 3lb., only 1lb. less than the backs put together, yet is as agile as a kitten.

> 'Chelsea's captain and goalkeeper was born at Wellington, Shropshire, twenty-nine and a half years ago. He stands 6ft. 3in. in height and weighs 22st. 3lb. Foulke is a veritable wonder, and his astonishing activity and goalkeeping ability have aroused almost a fever of interest in his doings beneath the bar for Chelsea. "Little Willie" played for England against Wales in 1897 and has gained two Cup-winners' medals. Sheffield United secured his transfer from a Derbyshire colliery club for £19. He has played cricket for Derbyshire, and his talent for directing a team is very valuable to the Chelsea Club.'

As a draw alone Foulke is worth his weight in gold, and the way he is playing at the moment proves him to be one of the best goalkeepers in the League. He stops low "daisy-cutters" and high dropping shots with equal ease, and his punch despatches the ball to a distant point of the horizon. He has accomplished many good performances this season, but perhaps his best so far was his fine fantasia at the close of the match against West Bromwich Albion. The 'Throstles' tried strenuously to equalise and sent in a perfect bombardment of shots, but Foulke was as imperturbably calm as he was adequate. The crowd gave him an ovation after the game.

The regular backs are Mackie, of the famous Heart of Midlothian team, and McEwan, late of Glasgow Rangers. They are reliable kickers and tenacious tacklers, and play together with a nice understanding. Mackie has a happy facility for getting in his kick, no matter in what attitude he may be, when the ball comes his way.

Key, from the Heart of Midlothian, plays half and last year got his cap for Scotland. Those who have seen him acting as a sixth forward and then assisting in the defence and generally making himself exceedingly inconvenient to opponents, are not surprised he obtained this honour.

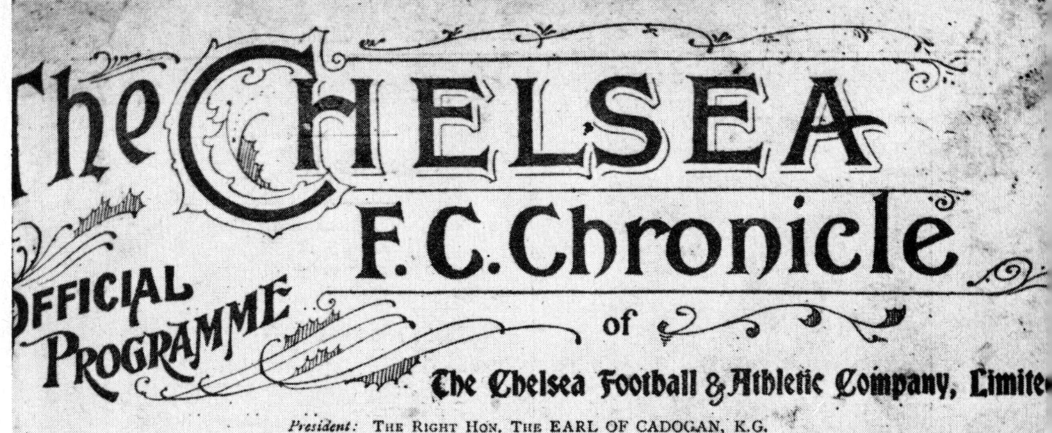

The Chelsea F.C. Chronicle

Official Programme of The Chelsea Football & Athletic Company, Limited

President: THE RIGHT HON. THE EARL OF CADOGAN, K.G.

Vice Presidents:
C. A. WHITMORE, ESQ., M.P.
COLONEL LESLIE POWELL, J.P.
C. B. FRY, ESQ.
W. HAYES FISHER, ESQ., M.P.
MAJOR W. F. WOODS, J.P.
H. VENN, ESQ.

Directors:
W. CLAUDE KIRBY, ESQ., *Chairman.*
H. A. MEARS, ESQ.
A. F. JANES, ESQ.
G. THOMAS, ESQ.
J. T. MEARS, ESQ.
H. BOYER, ESQ.
T. L. KINTON, ESQ.

Manager: MR. JOHN T. ROBERTSON. *Hon. Financial Sec.* F. W. PARKER, ESQ. *Secretary:* MR. WILLIAM LEWIS.

Colors: Light Blue and White.

Vol. i. No. 1.] MONDAY, SEPTEMBER 4TH, 1905. [One Penny.

DAISY CUTTERS.

"THEY'RE OFF!"

* * *

Racing men talk of "the saddling bell at Lincoln" in March.

* * *

Bah! It's at the "bottom of the League" compared with the first trill of the Ref's whistle in September.

* * *

Well, now what do you think of our Ground—and the stand—and the terracing? Good enough for SECOND Division Football, is it not?

* * *

And it is only a baby as yet. Wait until it is full grown, and then—well, we shall see what we Chel-sea.

* * *

Don't be over sanguine and expect *too* much of the teams at the first start. We don't expect to "stroll" into the First Division, but we *shall* get there in time.

* * *

One thing, we have a team of genuine triers, who are on the best of terms with themselves and with one

Yes, that is one of our mottoes. We have another one, which we owe to (and is typical of) the Father of the Chelsea F.C.—Mr. "Gus" Mears. It is "Don't Worry."

* * *

When the baby-Club, a fine healthy child from the first, was scarcely opening its eyes upon the world, it found—like all good children in the fairy tales—an evil genius, which took the form of a Dakoit, seeking an opportunity to destroy it. Good word, Dakoit, look it up in Nuttall's. We had some anxious moments, but the "happy father" merely smiled good humouredly and said "Don't Worry!"

* * *

Then we had some more anxious moments. There were many and vexatious delays caused by various formalities with the constructional work, and doubts were freely expressed as to the completion of the Stands, &c., in time for the season. Again the same cheery optimism and emphatic "Don't Worry!"

* * *

And so the expression has become our watchword, and you will hear it twenty times a day at Stamford Bridge.

Four pages for one (old) penny for the first match at Stamford Bridge, a 'friendly' against Liverpool.

Watson, another clever Scotsman, or Craigie, from Manchester City, generally play centre-half. Both are good, and I am the third of the line. I gained my experience playing for Southampton, Everton and Glasgow Rangers, and was capped for Scotland sixteen times.

The forwards are an accomplished set of players. They can play the three-inside game or indulge in those long, swinging passes out to the wings that are more effective against some teams. McRoberts, of Small Heath, is in the centre. He was the first player signed on by the club. He is a splendid shot, and when he does not score a goal a match one hears rumours that he is not well. But that is only because of his sad expression. Nothing is more cheering to 'Mac' than scoring a good goal.

Moran is outside-right. He made a big reputation while with the Heart of Midlothian, but has never played so well in his life as he has since donning the light blue jersey of the Chelsea Club. His sensational centres are quite one of the striking features of the game.

Chelsea Football Club.

SEASON TICKETS - 1905-1906.

PRICES:

	£	s.	d.
To Ground and Stand—			
Gentlemen	1	1	0
Ladies and School Boys ..	0	10	6
To Ground only—			
Gentlemen	0	10	6
Ladies and School Boys ..	0	5	6

Gentlemen's & School Boys' Tickets are non-transferable.

Ladies' Tickets are transferable to Ladies only.

What a Chelsea season-ticket cost in 1905. In those days 'seasons' were sold for terraces as well as stand.

Chelsea attack the West Bromwich Albion goal at Stamford Bridge on 23 September, 1905. The result was 1–0 to Chelsea.

Copeland, from Tottenham Hotspur, generally acts at inside-right. It was the Copeland and Kirwan left wing that played such an important part in gaining the Cup for Tottenham. Now Copeland means to do as much towards gaining promoton for Chelsea into the First League. James Robertson is a clever player and a fine shot at goal, and can also play in the latter position. Kirwan, the other member of the famous wing, still retains his old place for Chelsea. His partner is Windridge, of Small Heath. Both combine well together, yet do not fail to keep in close touch with the rest of the line. We have secured a number of other well-known players. Among them is McDermott, of Everton. He is regarded as one of the cleverest inside-forward players in the country, and several League clubs were anxious to secure his services. He first made a reputation when wearing the colours of the Celtic club, but while playing for the critical crowd at Everton he won fresh laurels. He is essentially a polished player, with a mastery of those deft touches one expects of an Everton player.

Another new man, who has a brilliant past and should have a still more brilliant future, is Pearson, of Manchester City. He plays effectively at centre-forward, and has the happy facility of being able to combine well with his wings, yet never missing an opportunity of threading a way through his opponents by himself.

One hears club managers on every side bemoaning the lack of forwards who possess initiative. The player who can get rid of the ball tamely whenever he is tackled and who always does the same thing every time is easy enough to find. He will never help win a Cup-tie or a League match. It is the player who can do things his rivals do not anticipate, and who is above all not afraid to shoot when he draws near goal, that we are all hunting for, and these we think we have found. Our idea is to have a strong body of reserves, so as to ensure Chelsea always having a first-class side in the field.

The Chelsea football programme, with its topical notes on the game in general and the Club in particular, has proved very popular. The two lads in light blue jerseys who throw up the ball when it goes behind have also provoked a good deal of comment and amusement. They form a striking contrast to Foulke.

My work has not been without its humorous side. Amongst the many applications for positions I received was one from a man who said he was a splendid centre-forward, but if that position was not vacant he could manipulate a turnstile. Another wrote: 'You will be astonished to see me skip down the touch-line like a deer.' A third was willing to 'be linesman, goal-keep or mind the coats.'

Lastly, it may be said that nothing is certain in football, and therefore no one can be sure of success; but, at any rate, Chelsea are determined to deserve it.

THAT FIRST CHELSEA SEASON

The first match Chelsea played was away to Stockport County in the Second Division on Saturday 2 September 1905. Stockport won 1–0.

Chelsea's first match at Stamford Bridge was a friendly against First Division Liverpool on Monday, 4 September, kick-off 5.15. Chelsea won 4–0, and it was fitting that Bob McRoberts, the first man signed by the club, should score the first goal registered for them. Indeed, he scored the first two.

On the following Monday, 11 September, Chelsea staged their first home League match and beat Hull City 5–1, with Jimmy Windridge completing the first Chelsea hat-trick.

In Chelsea's first season manager Robertson fielded up to seven fellow-Scots in his team—the start of the club's traditional liking for Scottish talent.

Back row (left to right): J. T. Robertson (Player-Manager), H. A. Mears (Director), M. Byrne, F. W. Parker (Hon. Financial Secretary), R. McRoberts, W. Foulke (Captain), D. Copeland, R. Mackie, J. Miller (Trainer), R. McEwan, H. Ransom (Trainer), A. Craigie, W. Lewis (Secretary), J. White (Assistant-Trainer).
Middle row (seated): M. Moran, C. Donaghy, T. Miller, Jas. Robertson, F. O'Hare, J. Windridge, H. Key, J. Kirwan.
Front row: M. Dowland, A. Slater, R. Wolfe, J. Watson.

Chelsea's first-season League results:

In date order, these were Chelsea's Second Division results in 1905–6:

Home

No.	Date		Opponent	Result	Score
3.	Sept.	11	Hull City	W	5–1
5.	,,	23	West Bromwich Albion	W	1–0
8.	Oct.	21	Chesterfield T.	L	0–1
10.	Nov.	4	Barnsley	W	6–0
12.	,,	18	Burnley	W	1–0
14.	Dec.	2	Burton United	W	3–0
15.	,,	9	Grimsby Town	W	2–0
17.	,,	23	Bristol City	D	0–0
20.	,,	30	Stockport County	W	4–2
21.	Jan.	6	Blackpool	W	6–0
22.	,,	20	Bradford City	W	4–2
24.	Feb.	5	Leicester Fosse	D	3–3
26.	,,	17	Lincoln City	W	4–2
28.	Mar.	3	Burslem Port Vale	W	7–0
30.	,,	17	Clapton Orient	W	6–1
32.	,,	31	Leeds City	W	4–0
34.	Apr.	13	Manchester United	D	1–1
36.	,,	16	Glossop	D	0–0
37.	,,	21	Gainsborough Trinity	L	1–3

Away

No.	Date		Opponent	Result	Score
1.	Sept.	2	Stockport County	L	0–1
2.	,,	9	Blackpool	W	1–0
4.	,,	16	Bradford City	D	1–1
6.	,,	30	Leicester Fosse	W	1–0
7.	Oct.	14	Lincoln City	W	4–1
9.	,,	30	Burslem Port Vale	L	2–3
11.	Nov.	11	Clapton Orient	W	3–0
13.	,,	25	Leeds City	D	0–0
16.	Dec.	16	Gainsborough Trinity	W	2–0
18.	,,	25	Manchester United	D	0–0
19.	,,	26	Glossop	W	4–2
23.	Jan.	27	West Bromwich Albion	D	1–1
25.	Feb.	10	Hull City	L	3–4
27.	,,	24	Chesterfield T.	W	2–0
29.	Mar.	10	Barnsley	W	2–1
31.	,,	24	Burnley	L	0–2
33.	Apr.	7	Burton United	W	4–2
35.	,,	14	Grimsby Town	D	1–1
38.	,,	28	Bristol City	L	1–2

Goalscorers: Pearson 18, Windridge 16, Robertson, Jas. 13, Kirwan 9, McRoberts 9, McDermott 7, Copeland 5, Moran 5, Robertson, John 4, Donaghy 1, Key 1, Mackie 1, Opponent 1. **Total** 90.

League Record 1905–6

P38 W22 D9 L7 Goals 90—37 Pts. 53 Position—3rd.

One year later Chelsea won promotion as Second Division runners-up.

Chelsea's original colours, those of their president, the Earl of Cadogan, were light blue and white. In those days the home club changed if there was a colour clash with the visiting team, and Chelsea's second choice was maroon shirts.

Chelsea's first board of directors comprised seven members: W. Claude Kirby (Chairman); Henry Augustus ('Gus') Mears (official founder of Chelsea F.C.); his brother, Joseph Theophilos Mears (grandfather of present-day Chairman Brian Mears); and Messrs. H. Boyer, A. F. Janes, T. L. Kinton and G. Thomas. The club's first secretary was William Lewis.

The first Chelsea F.A. Cup-tie was in the first qualifying round at home to the 1st. Grenadier Guards on 7 October 1905 and was won 6–1. At the next stage, away to Southern United,

Chelsea won 1–0, and in the third qualifying round on 18 November they were drawn away to Crystal Palace, then in the Southern League. On the same day Chelsea had a home League fixture with Burnley, which they won 1–0 while the reserves fulfilled the match with Palace and lost 1–7. To this day, that remains Chelsea's heaviest Cup defeat. The rules were subsequently amended to the effect that first teams had to be fielded in all ties.

In their first season, Chelsea finished a highly creditable third in the Second Division with 53 points from 38 games. The two promoted clubs were Bristol City (66 pts.) and Manchester United (62 pts.). United were as big an attraction then as they are today—their first appearance at Stamford Bridge, on Good Friday, 13 April 1905, attracted Chelsea's first 60,000 crowd.

The 'Move' That Can Make Chelsea Champions

BERNARD JOY ***(Evening Standard)***

WHEN the £5,500,000 redevelopment of Stamford Bridge Stadium is completed, the pitch will be moved 40 feet in a northerly direction and the stands on all sides will be much closer to the playing area. When that happens Chelsea will be as big a force in the League as they are in Cup competitions.

Chelsea have won the League Championship once, in 1954-5. It was an indifferent vintage that season, and Chelsea's points were 52, equalling the lowest total to win the title since the Division was enlarged to 22 clubs in 1919.

Yet few can match their record in Cups over the last decade. They won the FA Cup in 1970 after being runners-up three years before, the League Cup in 1965 and were runners-up in 1972, and the European Cup-Winners' Cup in 1971. They reached nine semi-finals in nine seasons.

The reason for the difference between performance in Cup and League is that Stamford Bridge is a 'neutral' ground. The remoteness of the spectators prevents a partisan atmosphere like that at Anfield, White Hart Lane, Highbury and Old Trafford, and to many visiting sides playing Chelsea at Stamford Bridge is little different from playing them at Wembley.

Former Chelsea and Arsenal forward George Graham, who is now with Manchester United, says 'Part of the explanation is that Chelsea have a cosmopolitan crowd who come to see a good game, rather than cheer on one team. Compare taking a corner at Stamford Bridge to one at Liverpool, especially the Kop end!'

Since winning promotion in 1963, Chelsea's away league record vies with those of the most consistently successful clubs in the period, Leeds, Liverpool and Arsenal. In nine completed seasons they won 72 matches, drew 49, lost 68. Liverpool's record was 68, 56, 65, and Arsenal's 60, 47, 82. Leeds were promoted a year after Chelsea and their vital statistics for eight

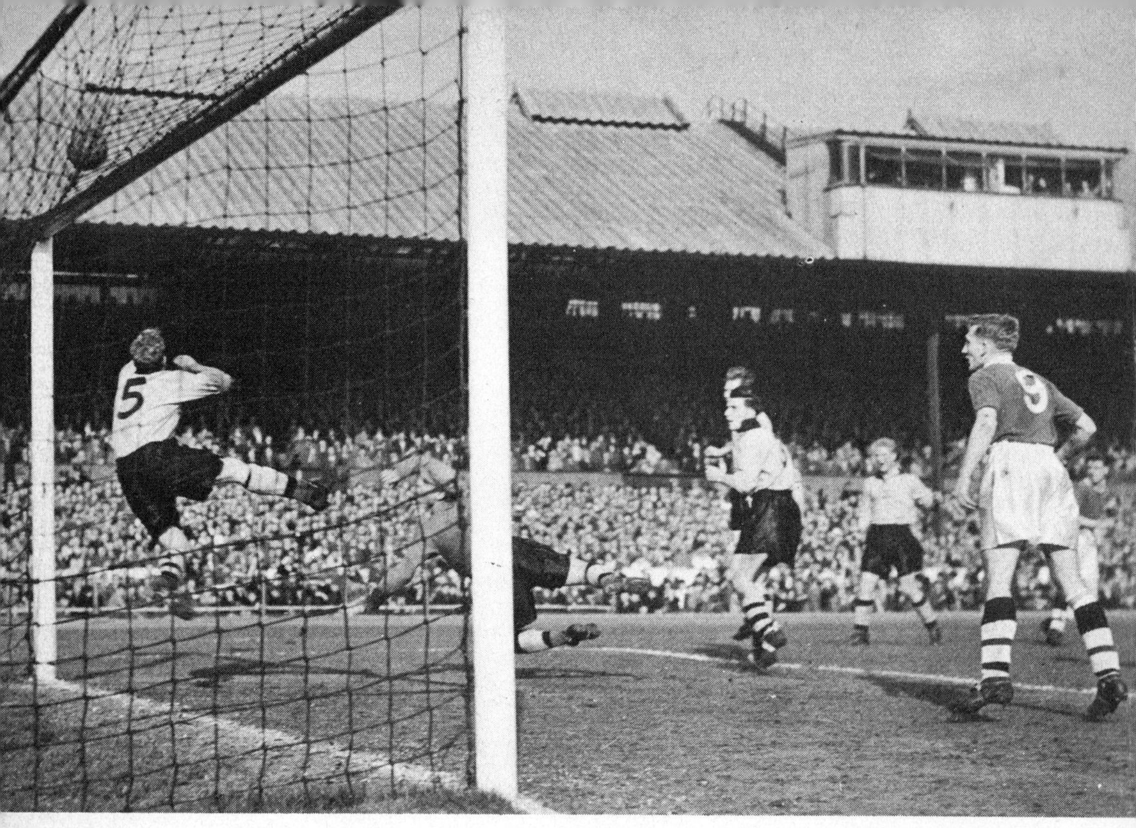

Above: Easter Saturday, 1955, was the day that virtually made Chelsea League Champions. Their closest challengers Wolves were visitors to Stamford Bridge, and the gates were locked 45 minutes before kick-off with 75,000 inside and nearly as many shut out. Says Bernard Joy: 'I can still feel the wave of indignation when a fierce shot by Seamus O'Connell was fisted over the bar by England captain Billy Wright, and for an awful moment the referee did not give the penalty'. This picture captures the incident—but Wolves did not escape. A linesman saw what happened and the referee, after consultation, changed his decision from a corner to a penalty, which Peter Sillett smashed past Bert Williams for the only goal of the match.

Opposite: A week after clinching the 1955 Championship, Chelsea visited Manchester United for the season's final League fixture. A wonderful reception awaited the team as Roy Bentley led them out at Old Trafford—United manager Matt Busby and his players lined up to applaud them onto the field as the band played 'See the conquering heroes come'.

seasons are 64, 58, 46.

When Arsenal carried off the Championship in 1971, they did so on the back of solid performances at Highbury. They dropped only three home points, as did Leeds when they won the title in 1969. Liverpool let six points slip away from Anfield in their Championship year of 1966. Had Chelsea's home points kept pace with the away form, they could have finished top in seasons 1964–5 and 1965–6.

There have been some fine away results in Cup competitions. When Chelsea won the FA Cup in 1970 they had four wins in a row away from Stamford Bridge—Burnley 3–1, after a home draw, Crystal Palace 4–1, Queen's Park Rangers 4–2 and Watford, in the semi-final at White Hart Lane, 5–1. A goal tally of 16–5.

In winning the European Cup-Winners' Cup a year later there were notable victories over CSKA Sofia in Bulgaria and Manchester City at Maine Road. In the final in Athens against aristocrats Real Madrid, a 1–1 draw was followed by a switch of tactics to a 4–2–4 formation which led to a 2–1 triumph. In the League Cup last season there was a very solid display against Derby on the Baseball Ground, while in the FA Cup Sheffield Wednesday and Brighton were eliminated on their own grounds.

In my playing days for Arsenal we relished a journey to Stamford Bridge, and most other clubs felt the same. In one spell in the 1930s Arsenal made six visits for one defeat and had wins there of 5–1 and 5–2. The trend was maintained immediately after the war, yet Chelsea had four successive victories at Highbury from 1946-50 and an even more impressive run of six wins on the trot in the 1960s.

I was so convinced that Stamford Bridge is a happy hunting ground for visitors that when I won the toss for choice of dressing-rooms in a League Cup semi-final against Queen's Park Rangers during the war, I chose the visitors', which was much more cramped than the home changing room in those days. My judgement was upheld when we won the tie.

Former Charlton goalkeeper Sam Bartram, who is a Press colleague nowadays, tells a story which illustrates even better the remoteness of players from spectators at Stamford Bridge. He says: 'It was a Christmas morning match and the sun was shining brilliantly. The fog rolled in from the Walham Green end and as we were attacking I lost sight of my colleagues. The referee stopped the match, but the fog lifted and we restarted. We were still on the attack when once more the mists swirled in. I could hear the crowd shouting, but couldn't see a thing. Suddenly a figure loomed ahead and I braced myself for a shot. It was a London bobby! "Your mates are all in the dressing-room," he called. "The match was abandoned five minutes ago." When I reached the dressing-room the other players were already in the bath, and wondering whether to send out a search party.'

Chelsea's varied fortunes in League and Cup have led to the charge that the teams are filled with 'big occasion' players, men who turn on the full power only for those games which take their fancy. Coupled with the charge is reference to the swinging life of the Kings Road, and the nearness of London's West End.

Dynamic right-half John Hollins says with justice, however: 'You've got to be consistent to win Cups as well as the League. You can't pick and choose the matches you want to play well in, because you can't turn your form on or off like a tap. Of course, if things are not going well in the League we obviously make a special effort to make amends in a Cup competition.'

Manager Dave Sexton echoes the sentiment: 'When we are at full strength we are a very good side. We have been unlucky with injuries over the last season or two but I can't pin down a specific reason for them. Our League record compares favourably with most and we have finished in the top half-dozen in

Chelsea 2, Arsenal 1 was the result of the first post-war League battle between these great rivals on 26 October, 1946. Bernard Joy, a pillar of the Arsenal defence at that time, is nearest the camera, with Chelsea's Tommy Walker on his left. Bernard recalls: 'I played left-back in that game and was given a rough time by Dick Spence'.

88 With Stamford Bridge in the throes of rebuilding and injuries reaching an unprecedented level, these players faced problems in 1972–73 that no previous Chelsea side had met. Back row: Steve Kember, John Dempsey, Micky Droy, David Webb, Alan Hudson. Middle row: Peter Bonetti,

Marvin Hinton, Peter Osgood, Ron Harris, Chris Garland, Ian Hutchinson, Paddy Mulligan, John Phillips. Front: Peter Houseman, Charlie Cooke, John Boyle, Tommy Baldwin, John Hollins, Eddie McCreadie.

Among the most memorable games in Chelsea's Championship-winning season was one they lost, 5–6 at home to Manchester United. Bernard Joy remembers it as 'a fantastic clash, full of wonderful entertainment as well as goals'. Chelsea led just once, at 2–1. Then United centre-forward Tommy Taylor (on ground, left) plunged to head this equaliser from a corner. Bill Robertson is the beaten 'keeper, No. 3 is Stan Willemse and No. 4 Ken Armstrong, with Ron Greenwood in front of him.

most seasons since we came back into the First Division ten years ago.'

Sexton took over as manager in October 1967, when the club was dangerously near the foot of the table, having gone six games without a win. He stopped the immediate rot and then built up a team of high quality. His recipe for team-building is this: 'Football is like chemistry. Players inter-act and improve each other's performance. If you find the right blend you are two-thirds of the way to success. I don't really blend the players, they do it themselves'.

He is bold in backing his judgement of a player and paid six-figure fees for Alan Birchenall, Keith Weller—both are now with Leicester—Chris Garland and Steve Kember. The original £80,000 fee for former Southend striker Bill Garner could also reach £100,000 if he wins international honours.

What a contrast there was in the way Ted Drake assembled

the Championship-winning team. He scoured the lower divisions for Stan Willemse, Johnny McNichol, Ron Greenwood, Frank Blunstone, Stan Wicks and Les Stubbs. In addition he called in amateur internationals Jim Lewis and Seamus O'Connell. He chose men of character and five who played in the League side went on to become managers: Ron Greenwood, Frank Blunstone, John Harris, Roy Bentley and Alan Dicks.

There was some wonderful entertainment that season. And no match was better than a fantastic clash with Manchester United. It was O'Connell's début and he scored a hat-trick, only to finish on the losing side. The scoring went 0–1, 1–1, 2–1, 2–2, 2–3, 2–4, 2–5, 3–5, 3–6, 4–6, 5–6. Drake telephoned scout Jimmy Thompson that night and said 'You should have been here, it was the finest match I have ever seen'. Thompson replied 'I'm glad I wasn't. I've just seen a schoolboy who will play for England one day. His name is Jimmy Greaves.'

There was excitement of a different sort in other matches. In a friendly at home to Red Banner, of Hungary, three penalties were missed in 12 minutes, two by John Harris. Chelsea obtained a goal against Leicester when two defenders, Milburn and Froggatt, simultaneously kicked the ball into the net. It is the only shared own-goal on record. And when Chelsea got on top of the Division in March, there was a newspaper strike so that the feat could not be blazoned in headlines.

The crunch match was against chief challengers Wolves in April. There were 75,000 spectators in the ground and nearly as many locked outside. Whatever the charge in recent times, there was no lack of atmosphere that afternoon. I can still feel the wave of indignation when a fierce shot by O'Connell was fisted over the bar by England captain Billy Wright, and for an awful moment the referee did not give the penalty. But a linesman had seen it, Peter Sillett scored from the spot and justice was done.

As I have said, 1954–5 was not a vintage season and that side would not have lived with the present one. But they had at least two players who would challenge strongly for a place in Chelsea's best-ever side. Roy Bentley had skill, physique and heading power. What a wonderful foil he would have been to Peter Osgood. Ken Armstrong was reliable, loyal, industrious but less dynamic than the present right-half John Hollins.

Men of character, and Chelsea have other players from the same mould who will, I feel sure, help them achieve results in League as well as Cup to match the fabulous stadium which is being built.

New Stars on Chelsea's Horizon

EVERY year Chelsea give trials at their Mitcham training ground to some 800 schoolboys—in age groups 12–13–14—to find 50 who are suitable for club training two nights a week. Of that 50, probably half develop sufficiently to become juniors when they leave school, and the ratio of juniors who are engaged as apprentices is four out of ten. In ten years up to the end of last season Chelsea signed 84 boys as apprentices, but on average only one in 12 reaches the first team.

That summarises all the sieving and sifting of players that goes on between the ages of 12 and 18. It forms a large part of each season's work for Youth Manager Ken Shellito and his assistant Eddie Heath .'Without looking you don't find', explains Ken, 'and you must look a lot to find a few. One jewel makes up for all the times you have to say "Sorry, son . . . you are not up to the standard we require." '

The jewels have been discovered at an extraordinary rate since Chelsea began their nursery season in 1947–48. Consider the following, listed in the approximate order of their first-team débuts: Bobby Smith, Peter Brabrook, Ron Tindall, Les Allen, Jimmy Greaves, Barry Bridges, Bobby Tambling, Ken Shellito, Terry Venables, Peter Bonetti, Ron Harris, Peter Houseman, John Hollins, John Boyle, Jim McCalliog, Peter Osgood, Alan Hudson. Last season's graduates to senior football included Gary Locke, Brian Bason, Ian Britton, Graham Wilkins, and Mike Brolly.

Locke, an 18-year-old England Youth cap, was pressing so hard for the right-back position at the start of 1972–73 that in September Chelsea felt able to sell Paddy Mulligan, captain of Eire, to Crystal Palace for £70,000.

Says Shellito: 'Paddy's transfer meant that Dave Sexton rated Locke at £70,000, too . . . which in turn means that Gary will have paid for Chelsea's Youth team for the next five years.'

This was Chelsea's 1972–73 junior team that reached the FA Youth Cup semi-final. Back row (left to right): John Spong, Jimmy McMorran, Paul Sees, Derek Richardson, Colin Harris, Steve Perkins, Steve Wicks. Front: Tommy Cunningham, Teddy Maybank, 'Butch' Wilkins, Ray Lewington, Les Briley, Mike Brolly, Brian Bason.

Locke has already been likened to Shellito at his playing peak, and Ken himself sees a resemblance. 'Though Gary moved up to the senior squad last year, he still comes to me for a talk. I can help him become a better player than I was by passing on some of my experience. Now that he has that season under his belt, I can't see Gary Locke looking back.'

Among other starlets who showed good potential last season were Steve Finnieston, a Scotland Youth International born in Edinburgh but a Londoner since he was ten, and Raymond Wilkins, younger brother of Chelsea professional Graham and known as 'Butch' to everyone at Stamford Bridge.

Finnieston is a particularly dangerous young man in and around the penalty-area. He is rarely off target with a shot, which means that goalkeepers nearly always have to do something when he is on the ball. 'Jock' keeps count of the Chelsea goals he scores, and by the end of 1972–73 had taken his total past 100 in three seasons of junior and reserve football.

Finnieston trained at Chelsea for two evenings a week while he was still at school at Woking. One of his teachers recommended him to the club. On leaving school Steve joined Chelsea

Graham Wilkins (left) aged 18, and apprentice brother Ray 'Butch' Wilkins, 16. They come from Hillingdon, and are sons of former Brentford player George Wilkins. They could follow the Silletts (Peter and John) and the Harris's (Ron and Allan) as the next brothers in Chelsea's first team.

Four ex-juniors who are now Chelsea professionals, left to right Keith Lawrence, Steve Sherwood, Gary Locke and Ian Britton.

as an apprentice. He made quick progress and on his 17th birthday signed professional.

Steve trains with the reserves. He is getting stronger and quicker, both mentally and physically, and against better opposition in the Combination side he responded well in the presence of experienced players like John Boyle, Tommy Baldwin and Marvin Hinton. He is working to improve his headwork, and at 18 looks a fair candidate for the First Division.

For a 16-year-old, 'Butch' Wilkins, an England Schoolboy cap, has remarkable talent. He is a midfield marshal in every sense; he tackles, directs pin-point passes all over the field and is aware of all that is going on around him.

In addition, he has the knack of making others play well. He gets them organised. Johnny Haynes at that age was regarded as a 'natural', destined for success. Chelsea believe 'Butch' is the

John Hollins and Dario Gradi supervise a schoolboy coaching session at the Chelsea training ground at Mitcham.

same type of player. He goes forward at the slightest opportunity, but tends to look for other players in better positions than himself. With coaching his appetite for goals will improve.

A tireless worker, 'Butch' made his mark in the reserves last season, which for a boy in his first year was some feat. He looks a fair prospect to follow his brother onto the Chelsea professional staff. Graham Wilkins is a full-back with the ability to play on either flank, good in the tackle and an adroit passer out of defence. Possibly he attempts to play too much football when under pressure, but this is not a bad thing in a young player.

England Schoolboy Brian Bason started training with Chelsea as a 13-year-old. He travelled up from his Crawley, Sussex, home two evenings a week, and as soon as he left school was signed as an apprentice.

Bason is at home on the right wing or as right link in midfield. He came to the fore last autumn, making his First Division debut away to Sheffield United in September. He has tremen-

Pre-match briefing for a group of schoolboy trialists from Chelsea's assistant-manager Ron Suart.

Ken Shellito, Chelsea Youth manager (right), and Dario Gradi, the club's assistant-coach, have a special word for former England Schoolboy internationals 'Butch' Wilkins (left) and John Sparrow.

dous stamina and a good shot, particularly with the right foot. At junior level he could beat players almost at will. The fact that he is quick and strong gives him scope for further improvement in readiness to take on older opponents.

Chelsea have never been afraid to blood youngsters. Says Shellito: 'Everybody gets a chance here. It's a young man's game these days and teenage players are becoming more the rule than the exception. The explanation is simply that young players of today are far better than we were. There are 13-year-olds training with me who can do things with a ball that I couldn't do when I was 17. They've got so much natural ability.'

But it is not only their skill which has improved. So has the role of the apprentice player. Shellito recalls: 'In my day as a Chelsea junior in the mid-Fifties, I used to have to sweep the terraces. We worked three weeks for every one in which we trained.'

Nowadays Chelsea operate a rota system among the apprentices, with two boys sharing dressing-room duty for one week at a time. This entails getting out the kit for training sessions, drying it and putting it away afterwards. They have to clean all the professionals' boots, also the footballs and mop up the dressing-rooms. It rarely takes more than a couple of hours.

On match days the two 'duty boys' work in Chelsea's dressing-room, before and after the game. The two boys whose turn it is the following week look after the visiting team at Stamford Bridge. 'This is a much better system. After all, the boys are here to learn about football,' says Ken Shellito. 'But certain duties are necessary—it helps to keep discipline and encourages respect for club kit and equipment.

'As in every walk of life, a boy will sometimes try to skip something. But all he is doing is delaying it . . . we make sure he does it when he comes in next day.'

Chelsea are among the clubs who recognise the importance of boys continuing their education after they have become apprentices.

'We encourage them to go on day release to college—for example, Steve Finnieston has been studying business economy —but it's not compulsory. To be fair, it is hard for many boys to keep up with college work by going only one day a week. I've found that only the really academically minded boys can cope,' explains Ken.

The boys are usually apprentices until they are 17. Then, if they have progressed satisfactorily, they are signed as professionals. But if they haven't advanced sufficiently yet still show potential, they can continue as apprentices for another year. Then comes the big decision.

'That's the worst part—telling a boy he is not going to make it. It would be nice if all of them could be signed as professionals but I'm afraid it doesn't work that way,' says Shellito sincerely.

Ken played 123 games for Chelsea and won one full England cap before injury to his left knee made him retire prematurely, in January 1969. He is in his fifth season as Youth Manager, having been promoted from coach when Frank Blunstone left to manage Brentford.

Less than three months after his League debut, 18-year-old Gary Locke sweeps the ball away from Everton's John Connolly with the authority of a seasoned campaigner.

This is 'school' with a difference, as more than 60 schoolboys with ambitions to play for Chelsea gather for trials at our Mitcham training ground. Some of those in the picture are now Chelsea apprentices.

Shellito came to Chelsea as a 15-year-old and has never wanted to leave. 'I thoroughly enjoy what I'm doing, and the most rewarding thing is getting players through to the first team. I couldn't wish for two better bosses than Dave Sexton and Ron Suart. They have helped me tremendously.

'I've also worked with, or under, former Chelsea managers Ted Drake and Tommy Docherty, as well as Sir Alf Ramsey. And I mustn't forget Dickie Spence, who is easily the longest-serving member of the Chelsea staff—he's been here since 1934 and is now Youth team trainer.

'I've tried to learn something from every one of them—to pick out their best points and incorporate them into my own personality. It's almost impossible, but I'm still working at it.'

Ken is a qualified F.A. coach, but does not believe the text book has to be obeyed to the letter. 'Coaching is like learning to drive a car. Once you have passed your test you never drive like that again. You have got to produce your own ideas. It's far better to sink or swim on your own ability than to keep looking at the text book for what to do next. In my job, what it all comes down to is the boys themselves. I couldn't have a better bunch.

Chelsea junior, Chelsea full-back star and now Chelsea Youth Manager is the one-club background of Ken Shellito, seen here in spectacular action against Everton in 1965.

102 Steve ('Jock') Finnieston, 18-year-old Scotland Youth International with more than 100 goals in three seasons of reserve and junior football for Chelsea.

I can honestly say I have not come across a bad 'un. That makes life easier. I simply treat them as I'd like to be treated myself.'

The juniors go on tour to Europe once or twice a year, and Ken says they are a credit to the club. 'We've never had any trouble—and that doesn't mean rigid discipline. It's just that they know how to behave.'

Shellito admits that he has learned a lot from the boys. 'When they arrive, some of them are brilliant, but then suddenly stop making progress. They can even slip back. At first I was terribly disappointed that this should happen. Then I realised that they have to adjust to their new surroundings and, more important, to growing up. Now I'm wise enough to know that most boys go through this "disappointing stage" before coming on again.'

Apart from those previously mentioned, there are other likely lads in the pipeline: among them 16-year-old left-back John Sparrow, who was seen frequently in the Reserves last season; Teddy Maybank, a South London midfield player; promising defender John Spong; and Stepney-born Steve Perkins, a midfield player successfully converted to a centre-back. Within a couple of years they could all be knocking on the first-team door. And the more competition there is for places, the better it must be for Chelsea's future far into the Seventies.

After the Cups and Cup Finals of 1970, 1971 and 1972, this is the story, in month-by-month diary form, of Chelsea in 1972-73.

That was Last Season, that was!

August 1972

Four-nil against Leeds United—what a start! Gates closed on 51,000 packed into the three-sided Bridge. Leeds are down to ten men after 20 minutes, with goalkeeper Harvey and Jones both off injured and ace marksman Lorimer in goal. Osgood scores in first-half injury time, Cooke bursts through for second, Garland adds the third and fourth. It's our biggest opening-day win for 22 years . . . our biggest League win against Leeds since season 1934–35 . . . their heaviest defeat anywhere for four seasons. One major snag, though—crowd chaos. Clearly Stamford Bridge under reconstruction cannot house 50,000 satisfactorily. Emergency Board meeting 48 hours later decides to cut capacity to 45,000 . . . considers fencing off terracing behind both goals to prevent further pitch invasions.

Next a 1–1 draw at Leicester and then, away to Champions Derby County, enter the 'Chelsea Giant,' 21-year-old centre-half Micky Droy, at 6 ft. 4½ in. and 15 st. 6 lb. currently the biggest player in League football. He is in because John Dempsey has damaged an Achilles tendon at Leicester. Wearing size 11 boots and shorts made specially to fit, Droy is the largest fellow seen in Chelsea's dressing-room since Bill Foulke, 22 st. goalkeeper in season 1905–6. Ron Harris bombs Derby with a 20-yarder (his first League goal for two years) and Chris Garland shoots the winner (2–1). Five point from three games in our finest start in six seasons.

Two home games follow. Bill Shankly brings his Red Army to Stamford Bridge . . . and you can't give Liverpool a two-goal start in 15 minutes and expect to survive, though Garland, scoring for the fourth consecutive game, makes a fight of it with a brave header just before half-time. Liverpool go top with seven points out of eight. They look Championship material. Three days later goals by Peter Osgood and substitute Peter Houseman

Chelsea take the long walk from the temporary dressing-rooms for last season's opening game against Leeds.

Harry's place! Trainer Harry Medhurst looks out of the £30,000 luxury caravan dressing-rooms that will continue to be used until new changing accommodation is ready in the £1½ million East Stand.

Last season's view from the emergency Directors' Box and Press Box in the N.E. stand.

Chelsea's big signing of 1972–3—Bill Garner, £80,000 from Southend United.

beat Manchester City 2–1, and in the last match of the month only Stepney's goalkeeping prevents us doing better than draw 0–0 away to Manchester United.

September

Away to Arsenal, Charlie Cooke sends us into the lead with a brilliant first-time shot. Thirteen minutes from time David Webb heads into his own net. Result: 1–1. In the League Cup second round we pull Southend's biggest crowd for years (24,160, with receipts of £10,038 nearly double their previous record) and struggle through a long second half to hold the early goal Chris Garland snapped from a half-chance. Next day Dave Sexton goes back to Southend to sign striker Bill Garner for £80,000. Says Garner: 'I didn't expect to be joining Chelsea. I thought it was West Ham for me, and was surprised when I got to the ground and found Dave Sexton in the office.' Says Dave: 'I have been keeping a close watch on him since last season. He is big, strong, powerful in the air. We need Garner to bring our squad up to strength. But don't expect too much too soon—it will take him time to adjust from Third Division to First.'

Two days later Garner is substitute at home to West Ham . . . and playing within nine minutes, when Alan Hudson goes off with a twisted ankle. West Ham play superbly, win 3–1 with goals from defenders Taylor, Moore and Bonds. Garner limps out of Stamford Bridge with his left ankle badly swollen; by Monday it's in plaster. A 0–0 draw in a friendly in West Germany, against Fortuna Dusseldorf, adds to the casualty list, so when Chelsea go to Sheffield United they have players valued at more than £800,000 out of action: Garner, Hudson, Dempsey and Houseman (ankles), Osgood (groin), Cooke (calf) plus long-standing absentees Hutchinson and Baldwin.

Brian Bason, a 17-year-old apprentice forward from Crawley, makes his senior début at Bramall Lane, where he won his first England Schoolboy cap two years earlier. Sheffield lead two-nil in 16 minutes and our one reply is Chris Garland's eighth goal of the season. David Webb is off with concussion from early second half. Next match, at home to Ipswich, he's dropped. Admits Webb: 'No complaints. I know I've been out of form.' Ipswich, second in the table, lose 0–2 at The Bridge (Osgood and Feely) while Webb helps the reserves win 1–0 at Bournemouth.

The F.A. confirm the two-year England ban on Alan Hudson (and Derby's Colin Todd) for withdrawing from the Under-23 summer tour of East Germany, Poland and Russia. Internationally, neither player will be available again until after the 1974 World Cup in West Germany. Chelsea transfer two stars to Crystal Palace on successive days—27-year-old right-back and Eire captain Paddy Mulligan for £75,000 and 30-year-old Scottish International ball artist Charlie Cooke for £85,000. Gary Locke, 18, makes his début as Mulligan's replacement in a 3–1 win at Coventry where Webb returns and Garner scores his first Chelsea goal but comes off second half with a ham-string injury.

October

The third round of the League Cup takes us to Derby again. No goals . . . three bookings (Houseman, Droy, McFarland) that are subsequently wiped out because referee Tommy Dawes retires after 30 minutes with blurred vision. We survive on cool, commanding defence and afterwards Peter Bonetti needs three stitches in a head wound received after only four minutes when diving at O'Hare's feet. Injuries to Garland and Droy in a 2–2 draw at Birmingham keep both out of the League Cup replay. In the season's finest match so far at Stamford Bridge Derby show their Championship class but Chelsea win 3–2 with thrilling goals by Steve Kember, David Webb and Peter Osgood's explosive volley—one of his fiercest shots ever. Under the eyes of Sir Alf Ramsey, too.

There's a shock for Chelsea supporters on 14 October. They arrive for the match with West Bromwich to find wire barricades 8 ft. high built behind both goals—the first time British fans have been fenced in. Explains Chairman Brian Mears: 'Since the season's opening game against Leeds, at which spectators ran on the pitch three times, our gates have been well down.

'I am convinced supporters fear more disturbances, and we have to show them that we intend to make Stamford Bridge safe for all. We have taken this step reluctantly and are not proud to do so, but it is very necessary.' Chelsea beat Albion 3–1 and Locke makes two of the goals.

Spurs 0, Chelsea 1 . . . and John Hollins hits a 20-yarder in off Beal for his first goal of the season. That's nine points from the last five matches, we're third in the Championship behind Liverpool and Arsenal, and the first club to reach ten away points in the First Division table. It's also our first League win at White Hart Lane for eight seasons. The right way for Dave Sexton to celebrate his fifth anniversary as Chelsea manager.

At home to Newcastle, Eddie McCreadie scores his first goal

 Dave Sexton: The rebuilding of Stamford Bridge and an 'impossible' injury list presented him with difficulties no previous Chelsea manager had faced.

since May 1967, but for the fifth time in six seasons the Geordies take home a point from Stamford Bridge. A 1–0 fourth round League Cup victory at Bury is to be Peter Bonetti's last game for two months. Early second half, he is accidentally kicked in the stomach as he makes a diving save; David Webb takes over the green jersey; Chris Garland scores for ten-man Chelsea (Ossie was off from the fifth minute with a ham-string injury); Bonetti hears we're one up, gallantly returns for the last 15 minutes, makes a marvellous save in the time added on for his own injury . . . and at midnight is rushed to hospital in Manchester for an emergency operation.

November

With John Phillips also injured, Bonetti's place goes to 18-year-old Steve Sherwood, 6 ft. 3 in. brother of Olympic hurdler John Sherwood. His only previous big game was away to Derby County last New Year's Day. Now he faces League leaders Liverpool and the Kop. Steve saves all that can be saved but Liverpool win 3–1 to complete the season's double over Chelsea.

Film star Raquel Welch, after a pre-match TV interview with Peter Osgood, enters the Directors' box at the home game with Leicester with a glass of wine in the right hand and Jimmy Hill on her left arm. On the field there is little to counter the distraction until Bill Garner thumps a header past Shilton for the equaliser. Miss Welch departs early, implores Chelsea ('I always look for their results, no matter where I am in the world') to win as she cavorts along the touchline . . . but the score stays 1–1.

To Southampton a week later. *The Observer* reports: 'Murder most foul at The Dell. For 45 minutes Chelsea dismembered Southampton with a display which cannot have been equalled by any team in the country this season.' But it's goals that count; Davies scores twice in the last six minutes, and from one down Southampton win 3–1.

On Wednesday, 22 November Chelsea go over to gimmicks at home to Third Division Notts County in Round 5 of the League Cup. McCreadie leads out a team festooned in blue and white scarves. They salute the Shed and West Stand, throw the scarves to the crowd as souvenirs, get on with the game and lead 2–0 (Osgood and Garland). More razzle-dazzle at half-time. No long walk to the caravan dressing-room; instead Chelsea stay on the field, suck oranges, change shirts, talk over the first half and go through a training routine for the benefit of the crowd. There's an unscheduled believe-it-or-not novelty in the second half as Ossie gives away an own goal, but Kember scoops

In October 1972 Chelsea erected 8ft. fences behind both goals—later the barbed-wire top was removed—and gave a lead that other major British clubs are likely to follow this season.

The League Cup-tie with Notts County on November 22 brought 'crowd participation' to Stamford Bridge. The players salute the fans before the game, then give away those Chelsea scarves. The gimmicks were abandoned little over a month later, having done nothing for Chelsea's gates.

the goal that makes Chelsea safe at 3–1. We're through to our ninth semi-final in nine seasons. The others: 1965 League Cup (winners) and FA Cup (semi-finalists); 1966 Fairs Cup and FA Cup (semi-finalists); 1967 FA Cup (finalists); 1970 FA Cup (winners); 1971 European Cup-Winners' Cup (winners); 1972 League Cup (finalists). 'Quite an achievement,' observes Dave Sexton with a modest smile that masks his concern over Chris Garland, who hasn't trained properly for two months because of that persistent groin strain but is still turning on the style when he does play.

Next Crystal Palace, complete with Chelsea old boys Mulligan and Cooke, come to Stamford Bridge. Much more pleasing than the 0–0 draw is the lunchtime draw on TV for the League Cup semi-finals: Chelsea v Norwich, first leg at home. 'It's the one we wanted' is the verdict of just about everyone . . . and the bookies make Chelsea 2–1 favourites to win the League Cup.

December

At Stoke, Ossie touches home Alan Hudson's centre for a fourth-minute goal, but Conroy swirls a cross over John Phillips's head in the second half and it's a point each.

Now the weather takes a hand in our League Cup fortunes. Stamford Bridge is waterlogged down the middle and the semi-final first leg against Norwich is postponed for a week. Hard luck for Ian Hutchinson—he was due to come back this night after 22 months out of first-team football with a cartilage operation and a twice-broken leg. But Hutch claims the headlines three days later when, by coincidence, Norwich are at The Bridge in the First Division. Dave Sexton summons the biggest strike force in Chelsea history: Ossie, 6 ft. 2 in. and 13 st. 7 lb.; Bill Garner, 6 ft. 1 in. and 12 st. 2 lb. and Hutchinson, 6 ft. and 13 st. The fans gasp at the sight of Hutch heave-hoing to the far post those long throws we've missed so much for so long; they roar as he smashes a shot against the upright early second half; and after Bill Garner opens the scoring at the start of the second half, they erupt as our comeback hero crashes two cannon-balls, left foot and right, past Keelan to complete a 3–1 Chelsea win. He leaves the field to a standing ovation from stands and terraces, collects a new £40 overcoat that, only days before, the manager had offered to the next Chelsea player to score twice in a match.

Four nights later Norwich return and displace Chelsea as League Cup favourites after an astonishing 2–0 victory in the delayed first leg. Compared with Saturday, big Droy is out of the Chelsea defence with a broken bone in the ankle; Norwich field the same eleven players but are a different *team*. Bone and Cross shake us with goals in the 11th and 13th minutes, and this time there's no way through for Hutch, Ossie, Garland or anyone. If only Garner had not been Cup-tied with Southend. If only we could have played this first leg on the right night before the League match with Norwich. If only . . .

Their manager Ron Saunders says: 'After Saturday's League defeat here, we had to come up with some answers. That Chelsea win taught us our weaknesses. Tonight we were once again the Norwich who knocked out Arsenal three-nil in the last round. We'll take some stopping now.'

Hutch's knee is swollen again. He misses the 0–1 defeat at Wolverhampton (so does Eddie McCreadie with a back injury, and John Hollins takes over as captain) and is also out of the second leg at Norwich. Starting two down from the first match, we're going to need something extraordinary to survive. Twice Norwich go further ahead, each time Alan Hudson replies (his only goals of the season). Norwich score again, and enter the closing minutes 5–2 ahead on aggregate. Wembley awaits them. Or does it, because unbelievably Chelsea survive the night as fog swirls over Carrow Road. Referee Gordon Hill takes the teams off for 25 minutes, resumes play for two minutes, then, with the touchlines invisible from the centre, has to abandon the game with Norwich only six minutes from triumph. Chelsea have begun the night needing a football miracle and finish it saved by an act of God. It's like Christmas come five days early.

Hutch plays against Everton (23 December) and John Dempsey returns, too—his first big game since Achilles tendon trouble hit him four months ago. Everton score two minutes from time, but big Ian courageously heads our equaliser. Peter Houseman joins the crocks with a pulled muscle.

Seventeen-year-old defender Graham Wilkins makes his début on Boxing Day in a struggling side beaten three-nil at Ipswich. Hutchinson is back for the last game of 1972, at home to Derby, and the substitute is 5 ft. 5 in. Scot Ian Britton, 18, rated 'a real little 90-minute buzzer' by assistant-coach Dario Gradi, who has seen him in all the reserve games. Britton 'buzzes' into début action after half-time, makes the pass from which Osgood dummies two opponents and shoots a smashing equaliser off the left-hand post. But afterwards the dressing-room is all gloom and Hutch is in tears. There's a lengthy medical conference about that right knee that 'blew up' just before half-time. After only four games, his comeback is halted . . . for how long now,

After long absence Ian Hutchinson scored three goals in four comeback matches last December. Then, minutes after this picture was taken in the home game against Derby, injury struck again and another cartilage operation was necessary. Have Chelsea ever had an unluckier player?

The moment that decided Chelsea's fate in the 1973 F.A. Cup. In the sixth round replay at Highbury, Arsenal's George Armstrong is toppled by Steve Kember . . . and then the penalty rumpus broke out.

we wonder? 'It will be at least three weeks before he can play again,' is the manager's bulletin. If anyone deserves a happy New Year, it's Hutch.

January 1973

Hutchinson enters hospital on New Year's Day for another cartilage operation. The news is held back for three days . . . until the morning after Chelsea have lost the replayed second leg of the League Cup semi-final one-nil (aggregate 3–0). So it's Norwich, not us, for Wembley. Peter Bonetti's return to goal after two months lasts only this one match—he's damaged ligaments in the left knee. At least there can't be any more injuries in Chelsea's next game . . . fogged off an hour before kick-off away to Manchester City.

One win in ten games is the poorest sequence of Dave Sexton's managership. Our first FA Cup opponents are Brighton, beaten in their last ten and bottom of the Second Division. We win 2–0 there, Ossie gets the goals and Dave Sexton, who lives at Hove, is home early for tea. If only Ron Harris had not been sent off (with Brighton's Spearritt) and five players booked, it would have been a satisfactory day.

Arsenal take both points at Stamford Bridge with a late and only goal by Kennedy. We go down 3–1 at West Ham. It's been a wretched month. Hutch, Houseman, Garland and Bonetti out, McCreadie in a back plaster, only the Cup win at Brighton to set against three January defeats. Dave Sexton says: 'From now on we'll give Mitcham a miss two days a week away and train back at The Bridge. It's been like some strange away ground to us all season with the redevelopment and one side fenced off. How else, apart from the injuries, to explain our poor home form? Yes, we've got to get used to Stamford Bridge again.'

February

It's Ipswich here in the fourth round of the FA Cup. Two-nil, both by Bill Garner, and his second only ten seconds after half-time is the killer. Great! Ipswich manager Bobby Robson's quote: 'I don't know why we bother to come to Stamford Bridge. We never get anything here.' Even this victory is clouded, though, by David Webb going off after 22 minutes with trouble in the left knee. The choice of substitute could not have been better—Marvin Hinton.

At home to Sheffield United, Ron Harris makes his 500th first-team appearance; in all Chelsea history only Peter Bonetti has played more games. Celebration takes the form of a 4–2 win

—two by Chris Garland on his return after five weeks' absence with that groin injury and two more by Garner. Houseman made two of them . . . playing left-back! It's a long time since Chelsea scored four—the first day of the season. But Dempsey's Achilles injury has flared again.

Leeds away next. Ossie scores our first goal at Elland Road in eight visits and it brings us our first point there during the same long period. A magnificent team performance, with John Phillips superb in goal. It's a fine end to a week that began badly with news of Webb having an operation for the removal of a piece of dislodged bone from the left knee.

Only two days after leaving hospital, Webb, stiff-legged and with knee heavily bandaged, insists on travelling to Hillsborough for the fifth round Cup-tie. Harris can play because, although he lost his appeal against a three-match ban for the sending-off at Brighton, he is making further appeal before the independent tribunal. McCreadie returns after two months—the first time he and Harris have been full-back partners in an FA Cup-tie since the night Chelsea won the Cup in 1970. Wednesday score first, Garner replies near half-time, and Ossie dives to head a spectacular winner from Hollins's free-kick. The end comes three minutes early for Garner and Wednesday captain Holsgrove. Referee Burns sends them off for fighting. It's the one blot on an otherwise much better Chelsea month.

March

Dismal stuff in the League: 0–0 against Birmingham, 0–2 against Wolves (both at The Bridge) and 1–1 at West Bromwich. Must be saving it for the big one: Chelsea v Arsenal in the sixth round of the Cup. All-ticket, of course, and besides the 36,992 crowd (receipts £19,085) at Stamford Bridge another 8,386, paying £1.80 per head, contribute £10,063 via closed-circuit TV at six North London cinemas and Shoreditch Town Hall. Harris misses the tie—the independent tribunal has reduced his ban from three matches to two, starting with this one; Garner, having used the appeal machinery to delay suspension for the Hillsborough sending-off, injures a groin in Cup-week training so is a spectator anyway. McCreadie, Dempsey and Houseman all come through a Wednesday fitness test in a practice-match friendly against the British Police at Hartley Wintney. Harris also plays there, although under suspension. The F.A. investigate. . . .

Osgood starts the Arsenal tie with a magnificent volley that is to be voted the BBC's 'Goal of the Season', but Ball and

CHELSEA 1972-73: RESULTS, SCORERS, CROWDS IN LEAGUE, LEAGUE CUP & FA CUP

1	Sat. Aug. 12	Leeds	Home	W4—0	Osgood, Cooke, Garland 2	51,102
2	Wed. Aug. 16	Leicester	Away	D1—1	Garland	22,873
3	Sat. Aug. 19	Derby	Away	W2—1	Harris, Garland	31,868
4	Wed. Aug. 23	Liverpool	Home	L1—2	Garland	35,375
5	Sat. Aug. 26	Man. City	Home	W2—1	Osgood, Houseman	30,845
6	Wed. Aug. 30	Man. United	Away	D0—0		44,482
7	Sat. Sept. 2	Arsenal	Away	D1—1	Cooke	46,675
8	Wed. Sept. 6	(2LC) Southend	Away	W1—0	Garland	24,160
9	Sat. Sept. 9	West Ham	Home	L1—3	Garland	34,392
10	Sat. Sept. 16	Sheff. United	Away	L1—2	Garland	24,458
11	Sat. Sept. 23	Ipswich	Home	W2—0	Osgood, Feely	29,647
12	Sat. Sept. 30	Coventry	Away	W3—1	Garner, Blockley og., Houseman	20,058
13	Wed. Oct. 4	(3LC) Derby	Away	D0—0		28,065
14	Sat. Oct. 7	Birmingham	Away	D2—2	Osgood, Webb	38,756
15	Mon. Oct. 9	(3LC) Derby	Home	W3—2	Kember, Webb, Osgood	26,395
16	Sat. Oct. 14	West Brom.	Home	W3—1	Osgood, Garland, Webb	28,998
17	Sat. Oct. 21	Tottenham	Away	W1—0	Hollins	47,429
18	Sat. Oct. 28	Newcastle	Home	D1—1	McCreadie	35,273
19	Tues. Oct. 31	(4LC) Bury	Away	W1—0	Garland	16,226
20	Sat. Nov. 4	Liverpool	Away	L1—3	Baldwin	48,932
21	Sat. Nov. 11	Leicester	Home	D1—1	Garner	28,456
22	Sat. Nov. 18	Southampton	Away	L1—3	Osgood	24,164
23	Wed. Nov. 22	(5LC) Notts Co.	Home	W3—1	Osgood, Garland, Kember	22,580
24	Sat. Nov. 25	Crystal Palace	Home	D0—0		36,608
25	Sat. Dec. 2	Stoke	Away	D1—1	Osgood	21,274
26	Sat. Dec. 9	Norwich	Home	W3—1	Garner, Hutchinson 2	29,998
27	Wed. Dec. 13	(SF1LC) Norwich	Home	L0—2		34,316
28	Sat. Dec. 16	Wolves	Away	L0—1		20,799
29	Wed. Dec. 20	(SF2LC) Norwich	Away	Ab.2—3	Hudson 2	32,000
30	Sat. Dec. 23	Everton	Home	D1—1	Hutchinson	23,385
31	Tues. Dec. 26	Ipswich	Away	L0—3		26,243
32	Sat. Dec. 30	Derby	Home	D1—1	Osgood	29,794
33	Wed. Jan. 3	(SF2LC) Norwich	Away	L0—1		34,265
34	Sat. Jan. 13	(3FAC) Brighton	Away	W2—0	Osgood 2	29,287
35	Sat. Jan. 20	Arsenal	Home	L0—1		36,292
36	Sat. Jan. 27	West Ham	Away	L1—3	Garner	35,336
37	Sat. Feb. 3	(4FAC) Ipswich	Home	W2—0	Garner 2	36,491
38	Sat. Feb. 10	Sheff. United	Home	W4—2	Garland 2, Garner 2	21,464
39	Sat. Feb. 17	Leeds	Away	D1—1	Osgood	41,781
40	Sat. Feb. 24	(5FAC) Sheff. W.	Away	W2—1	Garner, Osgood	46,410
41	Sat. Mar. 3	Birmingham	Home	D0—0		26,259
42	Tues. Mar. 6	Wolves	Home	L0—2		18,868
43	Sat. Mar. 10	West Brom.	Away	D1—1	Garland	21,820
44	Sat. Mar. 17	(6FAC) Arsenal	Home	D2—2	Osgood, Hollins	36,992
45	Tues. Mar. 20	(6FAC) Arsenal	Away	L1—2	Houseman	62,746
46	Sat. Mar. 24	Newcastle	Away	D1—1	Garner	21,720
47	Tues. Mar. 27	Man. City	Away	W1—0	Osgood	23,973
48	Sat. Mar. 31	Crystal Palace	Away	L0—2		39,325
49	Tues. Apr. 3	Tottenham	Home	L0—1		25,536
50	Sat. Apr. 7	Stoke	Home	L1—3	Ord	19,706
51	Sat. Apr. 14	Norwich	Away	L0—1		24,763
52	Tues. Apr. 17	Everton	Away	L0—1		24,999
53	Sat. Apr. 21	Southampton	Home	W2—1	Brolly, Hollins	19,699
54	Mon. Apr. 23	Coventry	Home	W2—0	Hinton, Hollins—pen.	18,279
55	Sat. Apr. 28	Man. United	Home	W1—0	Osgood	44,184

George punish defensive lapses with two goals in 90 seconds and it's an uphill fight. Hollins equalises before half-time, and twice in the last ten minutes Kember is so unlucky not to win it for us. Garner is fit for the replay three nights later, but Arsenal are still without Radford and Blockley.

They shut the gates at Highbury with 62,000 inside and 10,000 locked out. Arsenal have a breakaway goal by George ruled out because referee Burtenshaw is busy booking Garland at the other end of the field. Garner is winning everything in the air, and when he nods across a diagonal ball from Hollins, Houseman heads past Wilson. As on Saturday, we've scored first, but two minutes before the break Armstrong is brought down by Kember on the edge of the box. Inside or outside . . . that is the question? Burtenshaw, from the distant side of the area, gives a free-kick outside . . . changes his decision after a mass protest by Arsenal and consultation with a linesman . . . and Ball smashes the season's most controversial penalty past Phillips. Chelsea are on their way out. Early second half McNab breaks, crosses from the left, and Arsenal's winner is headed by Kennedy, the scourge of Chelsea in modern times.

The pursuit of honours is over for another season, but there are still ten League games to play. Garner's deflected shot earns a point at Newcastle (where an ankle injury ends Houseman's season). With Phillips in Wales's World Cup squad against Poland, Bonetti returns in the 1–0 win away to Manchester City, but Locke won't be seen in action until August, having dislocated his right shoulder while keeping goal in a training session.

Chelsea's win at Maine Road is Malcolm Allison's last game in charge of Manchester City. Four days later Chelsea visit his new club, Crystal Palace, who are in desperate relegation trouble. Palace win two-nil, and their first League victory over London opposition in 32 attempts since they came into the First Division in 1969 could be their last for another long time. An unforgettable month, yet a month to forget; that was how Chelsea could look back on March 1973.

April

Mike Brolly, an 18-year-old former Scottish Schoolboy International winger from Kilmarnock, makes his début as substitute at home to Tottenham (0–1), and keeps his place in the remaining six matches. That Spurs game is Alan Hudson's last appearance in a lean season. At home to Stoke, 20-year-old Tommy Ord, signed from Athenian League Erith & Belvedere last

In Chelsea's final home game the curtain falls on Bobby Charlton's wonderful career in League and International football. Chelsea chairman Brian Mears presents Manchester United's captain with an inscribed silver cigarette box before his First Division farewell.

Season 1972–3 ends with smiles and a cup—at Wembley! The prize is the *Evening Standard* Five-a-side Championship at the Empire Pool, where Chelsea beat Millwall in the final on penalties after a 2–2 draw. Left to right: John Phillips, Steve Kember, Alan Hudson, John Hollins, Tommy Baldwin and Peter Osgood.

October, becomes the 28th player used in first-team football by Chelsea this season (the most since 31 appeared in 1961–62, relegation year). Ord scores a beauty, but Stoke win 3–1.

Norwich end their run of 19 League games without a win, beating Chelsea by the only goal for two points that are vital to their First Division future. Another lone goal (a second-minute penalty) at Everton inflicts our fifth successive League defeat, in which sequence we have scored only once, and drops us to sixteenth in the table. Boyle collects eight stitches in a gashed shin.

Three matches remain . . . all at home over eight days. Brolly gets his first senior goal in the 2–1 win against Southampton, and Coventry are beaten 2–0 on Easter Monday. Hinton scores his first goal since September 1970 and the second is a penalty by Hollins—our first spot-kick in 65 matches since March 1972.

Only 18,279 are here for the Coventry match, but five days later the gates are shut with 44,184 packed inside Stamford Bridge for the season's final curtain. The reason: Bobby Charlton is playing his 604th and last First Division game for Manchester United before retiring. On the field Chairman Brian Mears presents Bobby with an inscribed silver cigarette box, but after the emotional preliminaries the game itself is anti-climax. The only goal comes on the hour, bringing Chelsea three successive wins, something they have not achieved all season in the League, and a final position of twelfth. Fittingly, on the day he is voted Chelsea's 'Player of the Year', the scorer is Peter Osgood. His exciting skills have shone through a long season of club misfortune and frustration; he has maintained his own style and standard despite ever-mounting casualties and consequent loss of team rhythm and confidence; he has scored memorable goals; and through those empty final weeks has given much-needed help and encouragement to young and inexperienced newcomers alongside him. In a mostly bewildering season of 1972–73, there could be no other choice as Chelsea's outstanding player.

The Big Match comes to Stamford Bridge

By BRIAN MOORE
(London Weekend Television)

'WHEN are you going to put Chelsea on the Big Match again?' is the constant cry of small boys with blue and white scarves. Last season, in all honesty, they must have been more than a little disappointed. Our visits to Stamford Bridge were few and far between. Certainly it was no ITV snub towards Chelsea. It was simply that while that magnificent new stand was being built, there was no way we could introduce the right sort of atmosphere into our Sunday afternoon programme.

Cameras pointing at a churchyard and a construction company's cranes gave everyone the impression that we were at a park game and not one from the First Division. We are as delighted as all those faithful Chelsea fans—and the players, too—that that is now a thing of the past. Atmosphere is vital for television football. You have got to be able to see a crowd and hear it in full voice. Without it you get the impression that you are watching a very Small Match, and not the Big Match.

I enjoy going to Chelsea. For the commentator, Stamford Bridge offers perhaps the best view anywhere in club football. There we are, in that spacious gantry tucked under the roof of the West Stand, exactly the right height above the pitch, exactly the right distance from the play, with room to move around and a clear view of the whole arena.

However, televising a football match goes far beyond the wishes and whims of the commentator. It's a massive production

Chelsea secretary Tony Green stands where the old East Stand used to be—after the site had been cleared for redevelopment in the summer of 1972.

The deserted background makes it hard to believe there were 51,000 inside Stamford Bridge when Leeds were beaten 4–0 on last season's opening day. Chris Garland scores the second goal.

getting the Big Match on the air on Sunday afternoons. For a start, I remember coming from a radio career into ITV and going to Chelsea with my producer Bob Gardam for a chat with the then Chelsea secretary John Battersby. John asked how many passes and tickets we'd need for our TV crew. 'Thirty-seven should just about cover it,' said Bob. I expected an explosion from J. B. . . . but it was no more and no less than he expected. As the new boy, it brought home to me straight away the size of the operation.

Cameramen, sound engineers, links engineers—who get the pictures from Stamford Bridge back to London Weekend—riggers, these strong men who heave everything into position, production assistants, catering men—yes, we do have to eat as well—floor managers, who tell us when we are on the air and off it, as well as the director and commentator. When you go to watch a game at The Bridge, the bit you see are the cameras. Two up on the gantry, one down by the centre-line that gets the exciting close-ups and one behind the Shed goal that gives you a different angle on the goals—always providing Ossie and company are co-operative to score them at that end!

My Saturday starts long before the kick-off. I leave home at nine o'clock to go to the World of Sport studio near Waterloo

Same match, Chelsea v Leeds, and a very different scene, with The Shed end packed to overflowing.

Football on the left . . . cranes in the centre . . . and gravestones to the right. The view the TV cameras did not appreciate at Stamford Bridge last season.

to introduce 'On the Ball'. That's live and brings problems of its own, so it's not until about quarter-past one when the show is over that I can really start to think about the game at Chelsea.

A quick drive along the Embankment—and there's Arthur, that genial man who guards the main gate, telling me where to park. Now the work begins to build up. I've got to catch Dave Sexton and the opposing manager to get the latest team news; there's a hurried conference with Bob Gardam to decide which players we shall feature in close-up at the start of the game. Then it's time to climb to the gantry and prepare for the kick-off.

On go the headphones and there's bedlam in my ears. The ceaseless instructions from Bob Gardam in the control room behind the stands are my life-line. He tells me the pictures he is going to show, when to comment and when to stop, whether I'm talking too much or too little and generally keeps me on my toes.

London Weekend brightened a dull game at Stamford Bridge last November by taking Hollywood screen beauty Raquel Welch to see her favourite team, Chelsea, in a 1–1 draw against Leicester. Jimmy Hill was the lucky escort.

Things are going up . . . and looking up! This was the progress Chelsea's £1½ million East Stand had made by the closing weeks of last season.

I'm helped still further by the monitor in front of me . . . showing the pictures that you will see on Sunday afternoon. I suppose I spend 50 per cent of my time commentating off the monitor and 50 per cent with my eye on the pitch. The monitor is vital, of course. There's no point in me babbling away about the brilliance of Peter Bonetti if what you are seeing is Dave Sexton, smooth and immaculate in close-up!

Within two minutes of the end of the game there's a live report for 'World of Sport', then a clamber over walls and barriers to get down on the pitch for an interview—anyone who has ever done it will tell you that this is the most demanding quarter of an hour of the week. A time to live on your wits, as you hope that the player comes to the microphone in time, fear that you will never hear what the programme director wants in all the noise, and for the most part freezing in rain or snow—but all the time trying to look confident and cheerful.

Incredibly, most times it seems to work and you come away pleased. Except that invariably the first thing your friends refer to is not the quality of the interview but: 'By heavens you *did* look perished.' I was, I was!

That night the match is cut from 90 minutes to something

David Webb, seen climbing here above Manchester City's Mike Summerbee last August, has worn every Chelsea shirt except No. 11. He showed his versatility in another direction one Sunday last season when, with Brian Moore hit by the flu bug, he introduced the Big Match on TV.

Scorer John Hollins and 'keeper Bob Wilson are both on their knees as this shot rebounds out of the net for Chelsea's equaliser (2–2) in the FA Cup quarter-final against Arsenal. In the background Peter Houseman claps—and breaks the silence of that East side.

like thirty by editors Michael Murphy and Jeff Foulser. The pieces for the slow-motion analysis are also inserted—and by one o'clock in the morning the package is all wrapped up and ready for the studio operation on Sunday. It sounds big and confusing; sometimes a vital piece of the jig-saw gets lost on the studio floor. But usually we find it in time.

My memories of covering games at Stamford Bridge are mostly happy ones. The welcome is always warm and the hospitality genuine. Some of the goals have been brilliant and rarely have the games been dull. Three seasons ago John Hollins scored the goal of a lifetime for us there and it won our Golden Goals competition; Roger Davies, of Derby, contrived the miss of a lifetime there last winter—again in front of our cameras. And I toppled over backwards in my commentary position when Peter Osgood typically scored a beautiful equaliser in that same game against Derby. Yes, there's always plenty going on for TV at The Bridge. But thank goodness we've seen the last of those gravestones and those cranes on the far side.